eat. drink. PASO!

Pretty Media Creations
179 Niblick Road #102
Paso Robles, CA 93446

ISBN-978-1-5136-1732-9

eatdrinkpaso.com

contents

menus

appetizers - 34

baba ghanoush - 35

black bean dip - 36

pimento cheese - 37

carrots with smoked butter - 40

roasted delicata squash - 41

burrata with grilled grapes - 42

rustic roasted veggies - 44

the warm goat - 45

buffalo cauliflower - 46

hash browns - 47

scallop and crab ceviche - 48

seared scallops - 50

scallops with bacon sauce - 51

calamari strips - 53

crab stuffed calamari - 54

chicken liver mousse - 56

chicken liver pâté - 58

cherry wood smoked duck - 59

roasted bone marrow - 62

lamb sliders - 64

pork belly - 66

wild boar bacon tart - 68

salads - 70

sunshine kale & quinoa salad - 72

baby greens & persimmon salad - 74

waldorf salad - 76

dad's caesar salad - 78

grilled caesar salad - 80

beet salad - 82

warm spinach salad - 83

crab & avocado salad - 84

ahi crudo salad - 86

brussels sprout salad - 88

venison carpaccio - 89

soups & stews - 92

kabocha squash soup - 94

cioppino - 95

roasted potato soup - 98

chickpea & spinach stew - 99

split pea soup - 100

chicken and dumplings - 102

beef broth - 104

bacon and lentil soup -106

mutton shorba - 108

cocktails (continued)

Here in Paso Robles, we are lucky to have so many wonderful, locally produced ingredients. When you make recipes from this book, if you are able to source your groceries in the Paso Robles area, try sourcing from these local producers & purveyors:

Boccabella Farms
General Store Paso Robles
Hartley Farms
J&R Natural Meats
Pasolivo
Pier 46
Spice of Life
Stepladder Ranch
Talley Farms
Templeton Hills Beef
The Groves on 41
Windrose Farms
Wine Diva Jams
YES Cocktail Co.

Chapter 1 - Menus

Entertain your guests with a menu paired with Paso Robles beverages. Here are a number of creative meals from a diverse group of chefs - try one with the recommended pairings for your next special get together.

ADELAIDA

ADELAIDA

Autumn Dinner
by Chef Alex Martin, Crush Catering

Cherry Wood Smoked Duck in Acorn Squash p59
Adelaida Pinot Noir | HMR Estate Vineyard

Goat Cheese Stuffed Chicken Supreme
with Oyster Mushroom Demi-glaze,
Roasted Cauliflower p119
Adelaida Anna's Red | Anna's Estate Vineyard

Baked Dark Chocolate Mousse p173
Adelaida Zinfandel | Michael's Estate Vineyard

Established in 1981, Adelaida Vineyards & Winery is family-owned and operated.

Named after a 19th century settlement in the Santa Lucia Mountains, Adelaida is located in the mountainous westside Adelaida District of the Paso Robles AVA. The estate property reaches 2320 feet above sea level and sits at the highest elevation in the region. This dramatic terrain has become synonymous with ancient calcareous soils of limestone and chalk, diurnal temperature changes of 40-50 degrees, and inherently low yielding vines with concentrated flavors.

Adelaida's legacy of excellence begins in the vineyards. The result is wines that show elegance, balance, and vibrant fruit flavors. Visit to tour the beautiful property, taste in their new state of the art hospitality center, or relax on the spacious deck while enjoying a glass of the wine for which they are known.

Open Daily 10am - 5pm
5805 Adelaida Road
800.676.1232   adelaida.com

BRECON
ESTATE

"La Crème de la Crème"
by Chef Alma Ayón, Sundance Bed & Breakfast

This menu of French inspired recipes pair wonderfully with Brecon Estate wines. The decadent meal is perfect when you want to impress your guests!

Seared Scallop with Orange Beurre Blanc p50
Brecon Estate Albariño

Filet Mignon with Green Peppercorn Cream Sauce p144
Brecon Estate Cabernet Franc

Chocolate Mousse Bombes p171
Brecon Estate Petite Sirah

Brecon Estate, an artisanal boutique winery located along the iconic Vineyard Drive, is a must for lovers of food friendly wines. After opening their doors in 2014, Brecon Estate amassed an unbelievable 70+ Gold/Double Gold Medals in under two years and has become synonymous with world class Paso Robles varietals such as Cabernet Franc, Albariño, Mourvèdre or Syrah. These stellar reviews are no surprise from Welsh Winemaker, Damian Grindley, who has a long track record of producing international, award-winning wines sold in high end restaurants. Production at Brecon Estate is hand crafted and sold exclusively on site. Each wine is fermented in small batches after being selected from their own vineyards or other high-end Central Coast parcels. Brecon Estate is home to some of the first Bordeaux plantings in the original Adelaida district. The stunning, contemporary indoor/outdoor tasting environment set amongst ancient Bordeaux vines, majestic oaks and a newly expanded outside seating area make Brecon Estate a truly serene place to relax, picnic and savor their exclusive offerings.

Open Daily 11am - 5pm
7450 Vineyard Drive, Paso Robles
805.239.2200   breconestate.com

CASS
Vineyard & Winery

Harvest Dinner
by Chef Jacob Lovejoy

This hearty meal finishes with a light, palate cleansing dessert.

Chicken Liver Pâté p58
Cass Rosé

Bacon and Lentil Soup p106
Cass Rockin' One Red

Red Wine-Braised Short Ribs p150
on Smashed Harvest Root Vegetables
and Braised Kale with Crispy Pancetta
Cass Cabernet Sauvignon

Citrus Granita with Agave p155
Cass Late Harvest Roussanne

Cass Vineyard and Winery is located in the rolling, oak-studded hills between Paso Robles and Creston on California's beautiful Central Coast. This area, that the vineyard calls home, offers quiet serenity for the visitor and an ideal growing environment for wine grapes.

Located on the East side of Paso Robles in the Geneso District, Cass Vineyard receives the evening's cooling breezes for which the west side of Paso Robles is known. They also rest far enough from the coast to generate the heat and low rainfall needed to optimally ripen the Rhone varieties grown on the 145 acre estate vineyard. In addition to tasting estate wines, the gourmet café can be enjoyed with recommended wine pairings. You are invited to sip their award winning Syrah on the veranda and enjoy a famous Benny Burger!

Tasting Room & Café Open Daily 11-5pm
7350 Linne Road, Paso Robles
805.239.1730   casswines.com

DRINK WITH EXPERTS

by Angela Payton

While we tend to gravitate to wine for pairing with food, this fun menu shows gourmet menus also work well with cider and beer.

Cheeky Cider Pimento Cheese Spread p37
Cheeky Oaks Cider, a dry hard apple cider

Cheesy Roasted Potato Soup p98
Majestic Surf, a West Coast IPA

Shaved Brussels Sprout Salad p88
Red October, a hoppy red ale

Pickleback Southern Fried Chicken
with Whiskey Gravy p122
Scottish Breakfast, an oatmeal stout

Brew the beers and ciders. Unravel the mysteries of wine. Study the art of the cocktail. Craft the perfect party. Enjoy luxury... hand crafted by you.

Master Brewer, Certified Sommelier with the Court of Master Sommeliers, and all around Bon Vivant, Simon Lynch has gathered his expert friends in an online academy where members perfect their passions or explore new ones.

Join Simon and friends as they teach, explore, and revel in the best part of being an adult. Come where adulting with style is the standard and where you, too, can Drink With Experts.

*To discover more about Simon Lynch,
go to
drinkwithsimon.com*

*To learn more about drinks, food,
and adventure, go to
drinkwithexperts.com*

from the pasture to your plate

FARMstead ED

A Rustic Dinner with Friends
by Lynette Sonne, FARMstead ED

One of the great things about living in the Paso area is being able to source all of your ingredients locally. This menu showcases some of the finest ingredients found in local gardens, pastures and dairies.

Roasted Bone Marrow p62
Tablas Creek Mourvèdre

Baby Greens, Persimmons & Toasted Walnut Salad p74
AmByth Estate Viognier

Prime Rib with Rosemary Salt Crust p146
and Rustic Roasted Fall Veggies p44
Rangeland Limestone Cabernet Sauvignon

Panna Cotta with Drunken Berry Compote p162
Paso Port Angelica

FARMstead ED's goal is to promote SLO County FARMsteading skills and practices via educational experiences, events and gatherings at pop-up FARMsteading classrooms held at local farms, ranches and Ag related venues.

The intrigue is for guests to have the opportunity to participate in classes in a variety of locations, allowing them to experience hands on amongst our locally grown and made!

The collaborative partners not only grow and produce their own signature products, they often cross-pollinate with each other to create and support new multi ingredient artisan provisions.

Annual happenings include:
 FARMstead Workshops
 Heirloom Tomato Festival
 Holiday on the Farm
 Table to Farm Dinners
 Pop-up Paso

For more information and a schedule of upcoming events, visit:
FARMsteadED.com

GLUNZ FAMILY
WINERY & CELLARS

Dad's Cooking Tonight!
by Joseph Glunz

No one in the Glunz family is going to complain when it is Dad's turn to cook. He has a few favorite recipes that everyone enjoys. Try this menu out at your next family gathering.

Dad's Famous Caesar Salad p78
Glunz Family Winery Viognier

Dad's Cheap Steamed Mussels Mariniere p114
Glunz Family Winery Zinfandel

Dad's Sweet & Simple Dessert:
A wedge of Stilton Gorgonzola or a good blue cheese,
a half dozen shelled walnuts, raisins and
a few unseasoned Melba toast rounds
Glunz Family Winery Mission Angelica

The Glunz family story started in 1871 when Louis Glunz, age 17, left his country of Germany in pursuit of the American dream. Louis moved from city to city in search of work until he arrived in the boomtown of Chicago in 1872. The American Dream was realized in 1888, with a business loan from Charles Wacker, when Louis Glunz was able to set up a shop as a wine, beer and spirit merchant on Wells Street and Division Street.

125 years and 3 generations later, the Glunz family established a beautiful winery and vineyards on Hwy 46 E in Paso Robles specializing in small batch wines from their estate and other select vineyards from around the Central Coast.

Open Daily 10am-6pm
8331 Highway 46 East
Paso Robles, CA, 93446
805.238.1400   glunzfamilywinery.com

GRAVEYARD
VINEYARDS

A Warm Your Soul Feast

By Chef Ryan Swarthout, Paso Robles Inn Steakhouse

Chef Ryan created this Winter menu to pair with
Graveyard Vineyards' Wine To Die For!®.
A menu designed to warm your soul!

Wild Boar Bacon Tart p68
Graveyard Chardonnay

Slow Braised Short Ribs with Creamy Polenta p152
& Roasted Heirloom Carrots
Graveyard Cabernet Sauvignon

Vanilla Bean Creme Brulee Cheesecake 163
Graveyard Estate Syrah

Graveyard Vineyards is a small family winery owned by Rob and Paula Campbell-Taylor. Located on the Pleasant Valley Wine Trail above the historic cemetery. Just six minutes from Highway 46 East and Airport Road, the winery is the perfect place to enjoy a wine tasting experience.

The award winning line of Wine To Die For!®, like the Sauvignon Blanc, Paso Tombstone White, Paso Tombstone Pink, Paso Tombstone Red, Mortal Zin, Dark Phantom & Deliverance are priced for everyday enjoyment.

The views from the hilltop winery are breathtaking with plenty of room for picnicking, lawn games, fishing in the pond & enjoying a stroll through the vineyards.

Open Thursday-Monday 11am-5pm
6994 Estrella Road, San Miguel
805.467.2043   GraveyardVineyards.com

Entertaining Friends
by Annie Browne, Hoot 'n Annie

Although they dine at local restaurants often, Annie likes to cook and entertain guests at home. Her passion for culinary adventure shows in this menu. Try these recipes the next time you have friends over for dinner.

Crab Stuffed Calamari p54
P.S. Cellars Arneis (P.S. It's Crisp)

Warm Spinach Salad with Toasted Hazelnuts p83
Broken Earth Merlot

Pan Seared Venison with Bacon Jam p148
and Gorgonzola Hash Browns p48
Polmar Junction Cabernet Sauvignon

Drinking Wine for the People

Matt & Annie Browne started their blog in January of 2010 with the original goal of tracking the dozens of wineries they visited each month. Slowly, through the magic of the internet, people started showing up and watching what they were doing - it's evolved since then.

At this point they blog about wine, beer, events, general lifestyle, recipes, life, motivation, adventures, travel, and social media. Most of the posts are focused on Paso Robles in the hopes that they will be beneficial to those reading who may choose to come visit this wine region.

Their journey changed a lot when their son, Sammy, was born. Rather than sit home and let their butts get saggy, they chose to bring him along and threeadventure.com was born.

In summary, Matt writes and is a social media consultant and, when not at her day job, Annie cooks and enjoys all that Paso has to offer. Needless to say they both drink!

Follow the blog:
threeadventure.com/hootnannie

THE HURRICANE
KITCHEN
THEHURRICANEKITCHEN.COM
FOOD THAT'S A FORCE OF NATURE
THEHURRICANEINC@GMAIL.COM
@THEHURRICANEINC

Game on!

by Richard Verhagen, Hurricane Kitchen

Chef Richard has included three courses loaded with unique flavor combinations in this menu. These dishes are very popular with his food truck customers and now you can make them at home to share with friends and family.

Venison Carpaccio with organic greens, fresh mint,
basil and raspberry vinaigrette p89
Four Lanterns Winery Grenache/Syrah

Smoked Rabbit Faux Pho with portobello
mushroom and mustard consomme
served on soba noodles p130
Donati Family Vineyard Unoaked Chardonnay

Bourbon Smoked Petite Pork Loin with
grilled pears, fig compote and ginger soy vinaigrette p132
Lefondusac Grenache Blanc

Known for his ability to land anywhere and cook up a storm, Chef Richard was aptly nicknamed, "The Hurricane".

The Hurricane Kitchen is a chef-driven gourmet food truck and catering service with a farm-to-table focus, using locally sourced, sustainable ingredients to create unique dishes with bold flavors.

Chef Richard Verhagen established the original "Hurricane" in Victoria, BC, eventually moving the business to Los Angeles, where it quickly became one of the city's most in-demand gourmet food trucks. Although grateful for his LA success, Richard sought a more closely knit community that inspired and informed creative, rustic cooking, and showcased local growers and artisans. He chose California's Central Coast as The Hurricane Kitchen's permanent landing spot, and in 2016, relocated just north of Paso Robles.

Landing at public and private events throughout SLO County. See the website's calendar for scheduled dates.

thehurricanekitchen.com
310.729.5943

Global Inspiration
By Chef Thomas Drahos, Blue Heron

Chef Thomas has created a globally inspired menu to pair with P. S. Cellars' limited production wines. Take your taste buds on a trip around the globe with this menu that is perfect for a decadent lunch or light supper.

Honey glazed carrots with smoked butter
and Rosemary flowers p40
P.S. It's Crisp - Arneis

Roasted tri color beet salad with basil
balsamic and goat cheese mousse p82
P.S. It's Soft - Barbera

Duck breast with soba noodle stir fry
and sweet spicy carrot relish p126
P.S. It's Silky - Grenache/Syrah

P.S. Cellars is located at the Northern Gateway to Paso Robles on the Pleasant Valley Wine Trail. Owner/winemaker, Lisa Pretty, selects fruit from the Paso Robles AVA to make unique wines, ranging from CRISP to INTENSE.

The tasting room opens to a large patio that offers the perfect place to enjoy a picnic lunch while enjoying the views. The patio and Upstairs Event room are available for private parties.

Book a stay at the Winery Loft to enjoy the peace and quiet at this lovely wine country estate.

P. S. It's time for a visit!

Open Saturday-Sunday 11am- 5pm
and by appointment Friday & Monday
13350 River Road, San Miguel
805.610.0905   pscellars.com

PENMAN SPRINGS VINEYARD

Catch this!
by Chef Chico Mora , The Catch Seafood Bar and Grill

Although Chef Chico is known for his seafood, the land lovers always enjoy his lamb chops cooked to perfection. Try this menu paired with Penman Springs wine at your next get together.

Calamari Strips p53
Penman Springs Rosé

Sand Daps p115
Penman Springs Dry Humour

Mahi Mahi p116
Penman Springs Meritage

Lamb Chops with Mint Jelly p135
Penman Springs Petit Verdot

The rustic tasting room offers a true sense of country charm. Owners, Carl and Beth McCasland, opened their tasting room in 2000, a time when Paso Robles was home to just 40-45 wineries. Back then the area was known as a premium grape growing area with unpretentious wineries. Wine lovers flocked to the area to discover the wonderful wines and learn the story of the winery from the owners themselves. The McCaslands have maintained that same atmosphere even as the area around them became populated with a plethora of new wineries large and small.

With the outstanding wines priced for every day drinking, the warm hospitality and the idyllic setting, it is no wonder Penman Springs draws visitors back time and time again.

Come taste the art!

Open Thursday-Sunday 11am-5pm
1985 Penman Springs Road, Paso Robles
805.237.7959   penmansprings.com

Ranchero Cellars

Ranchero Cellars

Shining the Light on Chrome
by Amy Butler

Winemaker, Amy Butler, created this entire menu to pair with her Chrome, a grenache blanc blend.

Ahi Crudo Salad with Hazelnut Gremolata p86
Ranchero Cellars Chrome

Pasta Bake with Meyer Lemons and Kale p112
Ranchero Cellars Chrome

Wine-poached Figs with Honey-Chèvre Cream p156
Ranchero Cellars Chrome

The Ranchero name honors the spur-wearing vaqueros of the old west, as well as the cowboy kitsch culture of 1950s America. Amy Butler's wine style aims to evoke the pastoral history of early California: old vines and dusty fields, shady oaks and goats and chickens, rusty tractors and wooden fences... because these things are timelessly authentic... and she really likes them.

Ranchero Cellars is Amy's reward for over a decade of winemaking for every kind of wine company – from the venerable and classic houses of Napa Valley to the enthusiastic Paso Robles upstart. It's a slightly quirky vision that keeps her passion for wine alive, working with interesting varietals and using both time-tested and cutting-edge techniques. She can do whatever she wants however she wants, at times drawing on her Davis education, and sometimes taking wild leaps of enological faith.

At Ranchero Cellars, winemaking is fun, like it's supposed to be.

Open Fri & Sat 1-7pm, Sun 1-5pm
PASO UNDERGROUND
1140 Pine Street, Paso Robles
805.423.3765   RancheroCellars.com

RIVERSTAR
VINEYARDS

Get Your Grill On!
by The HATCH

Paso Robles is the perfect place to fire up the grill and enjoy a dinner with friends and family. This menu by The Hatch restaurant is sure to impress your guests!

Grilled Caesar Salad p80
Riverstar Riesling

Burrata with Grilled Grapes p42
Riverstar Tempranillo

Hanger Steak with Citrus Pesto p142
Riverstar Affinity

Riverstar Vineyards is a family owned and operated vineyard and winery on the Pleasant Valley Wine Trail. This beautiful eighty acre property provides a warm welcome, great wines, and relaxing scenery.

Let Riverstar play host to you, your family and friends where you can taste the delicious estate wine, enjoy the company, and stay for the sunset views.

The gorgeous grassy knoll is the perfect place for a private event or a picnic lunch. Play a game of Cornhole, Horseshoes or life-size Yahtzee while you enjoy a day of wine tasting and delightful Central Coast weather on the beautiful vineyard.

Stay on the property in the vacation rental. Located within walking distance of the tasting room and only minutes from historic downtown Paso Robles, this is the perfect escape into Wine Country!

Open Thursday - Monday 11am-5pm
7450 Estrella Road, San Miguel
805.467.0086   RiverstarVineyards.com

SEVEN OXEN
ESTATE WINES

Dining with Friends
by Chef Tim Veatch

Enjoy this menu with your friends for a decadent lunch or casual supper.

Chicken Liver Mousse p56
Seven Oxen Rosé

Roasted Delicata Squash with Fromage Blanc p41
and Pepitas with fried Sage
Seven Oxen Grenache

Pork loin with Tunoto and Picked Red Onion p131
Seven Oxen Mourvèdre

Seven Oxen Estate is located in the rolling hills of the Templeton Gap in Paso Robles' Westside. The 130-acre property includes 26 acres of head-pruned, spur-trained Grenache, Mourvèdre, Petite Sirah, Zinfandel, and Tannat vines. South-facing hillsides, chalky soil, hot sunny days, and cooling afternoon breezes from the coast define the flavor of the grapes.

The vineyard is farmed organically by French Winemaker and Vineyard Manager, Bastien Leduc. Bastien began his training at an early age on his father's organic vineyard in the South of France. At Seven Oxen, he continues to work with a holistic, sustainable farm to bottle approach: No pesticides, herbicides or chemical fertilizers are used in the vineyard; yields are kept low to produce the highest quality fruit possible and to maintain the health and longevity of the vines; and a minimalist approach is taken in the winery to ensure Seven Oxen wines remain as complex as the natural environment from which they come.

Check Website for Tasting Room Hours
3340 Ramada Drive, Suite A, Paso Robles
805.704.0959   SevenOxen.com

~30~

TABLAS CREEK VINEYARD

Dinner Party

Tablas Creek Vineyard has created these four recipes specifically to pair with four of their favorite wines. Enjoy them individually or combine them for a feast!

Crab & Avocado Salad with Meyer Lemon Vinaigrette p84
Tablas Creek Cotes de Tablas Blanc

Pomegranate Glazed Pork Belly p66
Tablas Creek Counoise

Garlic & Herb Crusted Rack of Lamb p136
Tablas Creek Côtes de Tablas

Chocolate Truffles p169
Tablas Creek Sacrérouge
(Mourvèdre Vin de Paille)

Tablas Creek Vineyard is, at its roots, the story of a friendship between two of the international wine community's leading families: the Perrin family of Château de Beaucastel and the Haas family, American importers, distributors, and retailers since the 19th century. After decades of working together as importer and producer, they decided that California's Mediterranean climate was perfect for the traditional Rhone grapes grown on the Perrins' celebrated estate in Chateauneuf-du-Pape and purchased a 120-acre former cattle ranch in the limestone hills of west Paso Robles.

Planted with vines imported from Beaucastel, Tablas Creek produces estate grown, organically farmed Rhone varieties and Rhone-style blends including Esprit de Beaucastel, Cotes de Tablas and Patelin de Tablas, as well as a selection of varietal wines. In all cases, the winemaking is tailored to maximize the expression of the property's soils, with wines noted for their elegance, their balance, and their friendliness with the clean, bright flavors of the Mediterranean.

Open Daily 10am - 5pm
9339 Adelaida Road, Paso Robles
805.237.1231   tablascreek.com

chapter 2 - appetizers

baba ghanoush
by Megan Veillette www.fireandparchment.com

Megan recommends serving pita chips with this Middle Eastern inspired dip.
You can also use chips or pita bread if you prefer.

eat this with...
Barrelhouse Juicy
Firestone California Pale Ale

Yield 8 servings

5 whole medium eggplants
4 tablespoons Tahini
4 cloves garlic, finely minced
1/4 cup lemon juice
3 tablespoons extra virgin olive oil
1/3 cup fresh parsley, minced
1/2 teaspoon salt

- Pre-heat oven to 400F.

- Poke holes in eggplants with a knife. Set eggplants on a cooking sheet and bake for 25 minutes or until fork tender. Set them aside to cool slightly.

- When cool, peel off enough skin to get a spoon into each eggplant and scrape out the flesh into a bowl.

- Put eggplant into a food processor and process until almost smooth. Add in all other ingredients, process until smooth. Taste and add more salt if needed.

- Spoon dip into a serving bowl, garnish with parsley and serve with pita chips, pita bread or chips.

black bean dip by Megan Veillette www.fireandparchment.com

Megan adds her twist to this classic bean dip by adding Tahini and apple cider vinegar.
This is the perfect appetizer to serve prior to a Mexican dinner or as a party dip.

Yield

- 2 cans black beans, drained
- 1/2 tablespoon soy sauce
- 1/4 tablespoon Tahini
- 1/2 tablespoon apple cider vinegar
- 1 tablespoon tomato paste
- 1/2 tablespoon garlic powder
- 1 tablespoon The Pepper Plant Seasoning
- 1/2 teaspoon salt
- 1/3 cup cilantro leaves

- Put all ingredients into a food processor and blend all together until creamy and smooth.
- Top with Cilantro leaves.
- Serve with Fritos or your favorite tortilla chips.

eat this with...
Adelaida HMR Pinot Noir
Brecon Estate Syrah
Caliza Pink
Cass Backbone Syrah

pimento cheese by Ange Payton, Drink with Experts

Ange puts her own twist on this cheeky cider pimento cheese that is perfect on crostini, crackers or the chip of your choice.

Yield 3 cups

1 small to medium red bell pepper
1 tablespoon grated red onion
1 tablespoon Hard Cider
2 tablespoons cider vinegar

1/2 cup cider mayonnaise
1 tablespoon red onion, fine dice
1/2 tablespoon finely ground black pepper
1/4 teaspoon sea salt
2-4 tablespoons hot sauce
10 ounces mild cheddar, finely grated
8 ounces sharp white cheddar, finely grated

Pickle the Vegetables:

- Roast the pepper by placing it directly over a high gas flame. Using metal tongs to safely rotate the pepper, char the entire surface. (If you don't have a gas range, roast the peppers under an oven broiler set on high; rotate them with metal tongs so they char evenly.)

- Transfer pepper to a metal bowl and cover with plastic wrap. Let sit for 15 minutes. Use a dish or paper towel to gently rub off the skin of the pepper, do not use water. Remove the stem and seeds, then finely dice the pepper.

- In a gallon sealable bag, combine the diced pepper, chopped red onion, hard cider, and cider vinegar; let pickle at room temperature for at least 3 hours or refrigerate overnight.

eat this with...
Cheeky Oaks Cider, a dry hard apple cider
Barrelhouse Blonde
Lazzare Sauvignon Blanc
Tin City Cider

chapter 2 - appetizers

For the Cider Mayo (yields 2 cups):
- 1 large egg yolk
- 1/2 teaspoon sea salt
- 2 teaspoons Dijon mustard
- 2 teaspoons Hard Cider
- 1/4 cup cider vinegar
- 1 1/2 cups vegetable oil

- **Make the Mayo:** Using a food processor or blender, purée the egg yolk, salt, mustard, hard cider, and vinegar. With the motor running, slowly drizzle in the oil until thick and emulsified. Store in a lidded container in the refrigerator for up to 7 days.

- **Make the Spread:** Once pickled, combine the vegetables and the pickling juice with the mayonnaise, grated onion, pepper, salt, and hot sauce in a large bowl; mix well. Combine the cheeses in a separate bowl and mix well. Add the pepper mixture to the cheese and mix to combine. Let the mixture chill in the refrigerator for at least 1 hour or refrigerate it for up to 7 days before serving; it should be thick but still spreadable.

carrots with smoked butter by Thomas Drahos, Blue Heron

Smoked butter is very popular in Denmark. With the new trend in the USA to use smokers, this honey glazed carrot with smoked butter and Rosemary flowers recipe is sure to be popular.

Yield 8 servings

- 1 bunch of baby carrots (tops removed and scrubbed clean)
- 2 tablespoon extra virgin olive oil
- 1 tablespoon chopped thyme
- 2 cloves of garlic smashed into a paste
- 1/2 cup honey
- 5 cups of ice
- 1 pound salted organic butter
- Rosemary flowers (for garnish)
- Salt and pepper to taste

eat this with...

P.S. Cellars Arneis
Brecon Estate Albariño
Caliza Kissin' Cousins
Cass Marsanne
Glunz Family Winery Viognier

- Smoked butter: Light a fire in a lidded BBQ. Almond wood or red oak is preferred, the fire can be very small. Once you have a wood burning fire, in a separate heat-safe container, place half of the ice inside. Then place the butter on top of the ice; repeat and cover the butter with ice. Place the container with contents on grill at the furthest distance from the fire as possible. Close the lid and let smoke for ten minutes minimum. Remove container from the grill, then remove the butter from the ice water, and dry on a paper towel. Reserve at room temperature until you are ready to plate.

- Honey glazed carrots: Bring 8 quarts of water to a boil, season heavily with salt. Add the carrots to the water and boil for five minutes to cook carrots al dente. Remove the carrots and shock in ice water.

- Heat a cast iron skillet covered with a lid over medium/high heat. Add the olive oil. Once the oil is hot, add and sweat the garlic. Next add the carrots to the cast iron skillet along with the 1/4 cup of water and honey. Put the lid on the cast iron skillet and let simmer over medium/high heat. Remove the lid after five minutes and reduce the liquid until sticky and coating the carrots.

- Place the carrots in a rustic pile center of a platter of your choice. Sprinkle the thyme and Rosemary flowers. Off to the side, place three mounds of butter and swoosh with the back of a spoon. Serve immediately.

roasted delicata squash by Chef Tim Veatch

Roasted Delicata Squash with Fromage Blanc and Pepitas with Fried Sage

Yield 4 servings

1 medium sized Delicata squash
1 tablespoon olive oil
Salt to taste
4 ounces Fromage Blanc
¼ cup pepitas (roasted)
10-15 leaves fresh sage
¼ cup Canola oil

eat this with...
Seven Oxen Grenache

- Slice The Delicata squash in half and clean out the insides. Slice the squash into half moons and toss in the olive oil and salt. Place the squash on a baking tray and roast at 375F until tender, approximately ten to five minutes.

- To fry the sage, heat ½ inch of the canola oil in a frying pan. Once the oil has reached 290F add the sage leaves and cook until lightly crispy. Pull the leaves out and place on a paper towel.

- Allow squash to cool. Add a small dollop of Fromage Blanc to each half moon, top with the roasted pepitas and fried sage.

burrata with grilled grapes by The HATCH

This is a quick appetizer to make when you have guests arriving. The grilled grapes combined with the Burrata makes a lovely combination. You can also use herb infused olive oil for additional flavor.

Yield 4 servings

1 large bunch red grapes
1 tablespoon olive oil plus more for drizzling
4 ounces Burrata cheese
Kosher salt, to taste
Bread, toasted

- Rub grape bunch with olive oil and grill over high heat for 1-2 minutes, turning frequently. Grapes should lightly color and char.

- Plate cheese and grapes on wood board or similar, drizzle with good olive oil, sprinkle with kosher salt to taste and serve with toasted bread.

eat this with...
Riverstar Riesling

rustic roasted veggies by Black Bow Sweets

This recipe makes a hearty vegetarian small plate or beautiful side dish. In addition to the candied pecans from Black Bow Sweets, FARMstead ED recommends sourcing local ingredients from Windrose Farms, Talley Farms and The Groves on 41.

Yield 6 servings

1 Acorn squash, cut in half
1 Delicata squash, cut in half
16 ounces Brussels sprouts, cut in halves
Extra virgin olive oil
Salt, Pepper & garlic powder, to taste
1/2 medium yellow onion
1/4 cup pomegranate seeds
1/3 cup shaved Parmigiano Reggiano cheese
3 twigs Rosemary
6 tablespoons butter
1/3 cup lightly crushed candied pecans

eat this with...

P.S. Cellars Barbera
Adelaida Pinot Noir
Caliza Syrah
Cass Grenache
Riverstar Chardonnay
Graveyard Vineyards Petite Sirah
Seven Oxen Zinfandel
Windward Pinot Noir

- Preheat oven to 400F.

- Drizzle squash and Brussels sprouts with olive oil, season with salt, pepper and garlic powder then roast until squash is tender and Brussels sprouts are crispy - about 30 minutes.

- While squash and Brussels sprouts are roasting, lightly sauté onions in olive oil until browned. Once the squash and Brussels sprouts have finished cooking, transfer to serving dish, stir in onions.

- Brown butter and fried Rosemary topping: Melt butter in medium sized frying pan. As butter begins to melt, add the twigs of Rosemary. Once all the butter is melted and begins to brown, (reserving Rosemary twigs for garnish) drizzle over squash and Brussels sprouts, then place Rosemary twigs atop veggies.

- Sprinkle shredded cheese, pomegranate seeds, and lightly crushed candied pecans over squash and Brussels sprouts.

the warm goat by Ali Carscaden, 15C

This warm goat cheese by Ali uses local herbs, cheese and honey. She also sources locally made artisan breads to serve her guests at the wine bar.

Yield 4 servings

½ cup goat cheese (a local Chevre like Stepladder Creamery)
¼ teaspoon truffle salt
Local honey for drizzle
Fresh Rosemary or other herb as garnish (optional)
Fresh bread

- Turn oven on to broil
- Pack Chevre in small ramekin and place in broiler until top turn golden.
- Remove from broiler and sprinkle truffle salt on top. Drizzle with honey. For added flavor, add herbs as garnish.
- Serve with bread or crackers.

eat this with...

Brecon Estate Syrah
Caliza Syrah
Cass Grenache
Pear Valley Syrah
Riverstar Rosé
Seven Oxen Cassidy
Tablas Creek Rosé
Windward Pinot Noir

chapter 2 - appetizers

buffalo cauliflower
by Annie Browne, Hoot 'n Annie

Annie has taken the classic buffalo wing recipe and made a much healthier version. Cauliflower, instead of chicken, works well in this fun appetizer.

Yield 6 servings

1 head of cauliflower, cut into bite size pieces
½ cup hot buffalo sauce (store bought is fine)
¼ cup olive oil
Garlic salt to taste

Celery, cut into sticks
¼ cup ranch dressing

- Pre-heat oven to 450F.

- Place all ingredients in a Ziploc bag and shake - be sure all cauliflower is coated.

- Spread coated cauliflower on a large cookie sheet and bake for approximately 20 minutes or until the cauliflower starts to brown.

- Serve with celery sticks and ranch dressing for dipping.

eat this with...
Barrelhouse Sunny Days
Firestone 805
Firestone Easy Jack

hash browns by Annie Browne, Hoot 'n Annie

The recipe for red potato Gorgonzola hash browns makes a nice small plate as an appetizer, or to serve as side dish.

eat this with...
> Brecon Estate Petite Sirah
> Graveyard Scream
> Penman Springs Petite Sirah
> P.S. Cellars Cabernet Sauvignon
> Robert Hall Merlot

Yield 4 servings

4 medium red potatoes, washed and scrubbed
½ cup crumbled gorgonzola cheese
Salt and pepper, to taste
Olive oil for cooking (or bacon fat)

- Grate potatoes into a medium bowl. Rinse and drain the grated potato 3 times to remove starch. Pat the potatoes dry and lay out on paper towels and let sit.

- In a medium skillet, heat the oil over medium heat. Add the potato slowly, in piles and press each down to form a patty about 3 inches across. Season with salt and pepper.

- Keep an eye on the underside by carefully lifting to see if the potato is browning. When it's golden brown, carefully flip the hash browns.

- Carefully sprinkle the crumbled gorgonzola on the browned side while the uncooked side is browning. When the second side is golden brown, remove the hash brown.

scallop and crab ceviche by Lisa Pretty

Serve this ceviche in shot glasses, on small lettuce petals, or in a large bowl with chips to dip. If serving at a party, be sure to keep the ceviche cool.

Yield 4 servings

4 large scallops, chopped in ½ inch pieces
2 crab legs, shell removed and chopped
Fresh juice from 8 large limes
½ red bell pepper, seeded and diced
1 jalapeno, seeded and diced
½ small seedless cucumber
1 teaspoon hot chili sauce
Salt, to taste
Fresh basil leaves for garnish

- Place scallops and crab in a glass bowl with a lid. Cover seafood with lime juice. Place lid on bowl and allow the seafood to "cook" in the juice, in the refrigerator for 3 hours. Stirring every hour.

- Remove from refrigerator and add in the peppers, cucumber, chili sauce and season with salt. Scoop the ceviche into serving container, including some juice.

- Garnish with basil leaves.

eat this with...
Brecon Estate Albariño
JUSTIN Viognier
P.S. Cellars Arneis
Ranchero Cellars Viognier

seared scallops by Chef Alma Ayón, Sundance Bed & Breakfast

These Seared Scallops with Orange Beurre Blanc, by Chef Alma, are a crowd pleaser at Brecon Estate winemaker dinners. They don't take long to make and have a beautiful presentation.

For the orange beurre blanc: Dice butter into small cubes and keep cold. In a sauté pan add wine, orange juice, shallots and cream; using medium heat bring to a simmer. Reduce liquid to about one third. Reduce heat to low. Swirl half of the butter cubes until fully incorporated; then swirl the second half of butter until fully incorporated. Keep the pan in constant motion so that the emulsion does not destabilize. Add kosher salt and ground pepper as needed along with lemon juice, strain and hold in a thermos.

For the scallops: Pat the scallops dry with paper towels and season with salt and pepper. Heat a portion of the butter and olive oil (1 tablespoon each) over high heat in sauté pan. Once the butter/oil is hot, add the scallops. Cook on one side until golden brown without disturbing (about two minutes). They should release from the pan when they are properly seared. Turn them over and cook them on the other side until golden brown. They should still be soft in the center when you touch. Do not overcook. Let scallops rest on a paper towel lined dish for about two minutes before plating.

To serve: On a warm plate, pool the beurre blanc in a circle. Place one scallop in the center. Drizzle high quality olive oil in a circular motion around the scallop. Garnish with chopped chives.

Yield 4-6 servings

4 to 6 U-10 sea scallops, cleaned
Kosher salt and pepper, as needed
Olive oil, as needed
Butter, as needed
4 ounces Brecon Albariño
8 ounces orange juice
2 shallots, finely chopped
12 ounces butter, cubed and cold
4 ounces cream
Lemon juice, as needed
Chives, finely chopped
High quality olive oil

eat this with...
Brecon Estate Albariño

scallops with bacon sauce by Andre Averseng, Paso Terra

This recipe for scallops with roasted garlic and bacon sauce served on pea puree is very typical of the dishes Chef Andre serves at his Paso Terra restaurant. French style seafood dishes are his specialty.

Yield 4 servings

1 ounce grape seed oil
1/2 cup flour
8 large scallops
1 shallot, chopped fine
1/2 cup white wine
4 ounces heavy cream
2 ounces bacon bits
4 cloves garlic, roasted and smashed
Juice of 1/2 lemon
Salt and pepper, to taste

Pea Puree

1/2 medium onion, diced
1 ounce butter
8 ounces peas
1 large russet potato, sliced
3 ounces heavy cream
Salt and white pepper, to taste

- For pea puree: Sweat onion in butter over medium high heat. Add fresh peas. Stir well until peas are tender. Add sliced potato and cream, reduce heat to low and cover. Allow to simmer until potato is cooked. Keep an eye on the evaporation and add additional cream if needed. When the potato is cooked, the liquid should be absorbed by the mixture. Puree in a food processor and season to taste. Keep warm until ready to use.

- Season scallops and dredge in flour. Sauté in hot oil in a sauté pan, 1 minute on each side and remove. Add shallot and wine, cooking until wine reduces by half. Stir in the bacon and garlic, then add the cream. Allow the sauce to thicken and then season to taste and add lemon juice.

- Place the pea puree on a plate, set scallops on the puree and then top with the sauce

eat this with...
Brecon Estate Albariño
Cass Rousanne
Castoro Rosato
Glunz Family Viognier
Graveyard Tombstone Pink
JUSTIN Viognier
Riverstar Riesling
Tablas Creek Dianthus
Windward Pintt Noir

calamari strips by Chico Mora, The Catch Seafood Bar and Grill

This recipe calls for a calamari steak to be breaded and pan fried. Feel free to serve with your favorite sauce, Chef Chico recommends offering a choice of tartar or cocktail sauce for dipping.

eat this with...
Penman Springs Rosé

Yield 4 servings

> 2 calamari steaks
> 3 tablespoons all purpose flour
> Salt and pepper, to taste
> 1 large egg
> 3 tablespoons Panko bread crumbs
> 3 tablespoons clarified butter

- Bread the calamari: Prepare 3 shallow dishes: one for the flour (whisk in the salt and pepper), one for the egg, and one for the bread crumbs. Beat the egg lightly. Dip one steak at a time, first in the flour, then in the egg. Let the excess egg drip off before coating the steak in the bread crumbs. Turn the steak to coat both sides with bread crumbs.

- In a large frying pan, heat the clarified butter over high heat. Add the calamari steaks to the pan and fry 1 minute on each side.

- Remove from pan and slice. Serve with lemon wedge and your choice of sauce for dipping.

crab stuffed calamari by Annie Browne, Hoot 'n Annie

These crab stuffed calamari appetizers can be cooked on the grill or sautéed in a mix of olive oil and butter. Either way they are delicious -- be sure not to overcook the calamari or it can be chewy.

Yield 4 servings

10-12 whole calamari, cleaned, tentacles removed
1 pound can of quality crab meat
1 bunch Italian parsley, chopped
    (reserve some for garnish)
½ onion, chopped fine
3 cloves garlic, chopped fine
2 whole eggs
Salt and pepper, to taste

Optional: 1 tablespoon olive oil + 1 tablespoon butter

- In a large bowl, mix all ingredients except the calamari.

- On a large work surface, lay out the tubes and carefully stuff them with the mixture with a small spoon or your hands.

- When they're all stuffed, place on the grill over medium heat. Grill about 2 minutes on each side. Alternatively, they can be cooked in a sauté pan, in melted butter and olive oil along with the tentacles.

- Garnish with reserved parsley

eat this with...
Brecon Estate Albariño
Cass Marsanne
JUSTIN Viognier
P.S. Cellars Arncis
Pear Valley Chenin Blanc
Pomar Junction Viognier
Riverstar Riesling
Vina Robles White 4

chicken liver mousse by Chef Tim Veatch

Serve this chicken liver mousse with Rosemary crackers and roasted onions.

Yield serves 6
- ½ **pound liver (Cured)**
- ¼ **cup Whiskey**
- ½ **cup onion**
- 1 **clove of garlic**
- ½ **cup butter (room temp)**
- ½ **cup cream (room temp)**
- 1 **egg**

Cure:
- ½ **teaspoon salt**
- ¼ **teaspoon pink salt**
- ½ **teaspoon white pepper**
- ½ **tablespoon 4 spice**

eat this with...
Seven Oxen Rosé

- Using a sharp knife, scrap the veins out of the livers. Toss the liver in the prepared cure and refrigerate over night.

- Mince the onion, garlic and sweat over medium heat with olive oil. Off the heat, deglaze with a ¼ cup of whiskey. Place over the heat and light the whisky with a match and allow the alcohol to burn off.

- Allow mixture to cool. In a blender add the whiskey, garlic, onion mixture, and cream. Blend until smooth, add the butter and blend until emulsified. Blend in the single egg until just combined.

- Pour in to 4 ounce ramekin or tempered glass jars. Place jars into a baking pan and fill the baking pan with hot water halfway up the jars. Place in the oven at 325F until just set or 165 degrees in the middle.

eat this with...
Cass Rosé

chicken liver pâté by Chef Jacob, Cass Café

The buttermilk soaked livers with herbs and Cognac make a delicious appetizer or small plate. Don't forget the pickles!

Yield 4 servings

- 1 pound fresh chicken livers
- 1 cup buttermilk
- 1 stick chilled butter, cut into pieces
- 1 cup chopped sweet onion
- 3 cloves garlic, minced
- 2 bay leaves

- 1 teaspoon fresh thyme leaves, chopped
- ¾ teaspoon Kosher salt
- ¾ teaspoon fresh cracked pepper
- ¼ cup Cognac
- ¼ sprig lavendar
- 2 chives, chopped
- Cornichons, or other sweet pickle
- Pullman toast points

- Clean the livers by separating the lobes and removing any veins, fat, or sinew. Careful not to squish the livers, as they're very fragile. Culinary scissors or a sharp paring knife works best.

- Soak the cleaned livers in the buttermilk, covered in the fridge, for 2 hours. Then, drain well and pat dry.

- In a large sauté pan, melt ¼ of the stick of butter, then add the onions. Sauté them until translucent, 3-4 minutes, then add the garlic and sauté for another minute. Next, add the livers, bay leaves, thyme, salt, and pepper and continue to cook until the livers are browned on all sides but still slightly pink on the inside. Add the cognac and continue to cook until nearly all of the liquid has evaporated and the livers are fully cooked. Remove from the heat and let them sit for a few minutes to cool down slightly. Discard the bay leaves before moving on.

- Place the warm liver mixture in the food processor and puree. Working in batches, add the chilled butter and pulse a few times, just to incorporate. Double check your seasoning, and add additional salt and/or pepper to your desired taste. To serve, pack a 4 ounce buttered ramekin with pate, then run the edge of a sharp knife around the edge before inverting it onto the center of a plate. Garnish with chives and lavender, the cornichons, and the toast points. Serve with a butter knife for spreading.

cherry wood smoked duck by Chef Alex, Crush Catering

Cherry Wood Smoked Duck served in a roasted acorn squash with melted leeks, sunny side up duck egg, and truffle salt makes a beautiful dish. Create this for a special occasion.

Yield 2 servings

1 (5-6 lb) duck
2 tablespoons sea salt
1 small onion, peeled and quartered
1 orange
1 bunch fresh Rosemary
Acorn squash
2 tablespoons olive oil
2 tablespoons salted butter
1 leek (cleaned and sliced)
2 duck eggs, cooked sunny side up
Truffle salt to finish eggs

Prepare Smoked Duck:

- Light your smoker and soak your wood chips in your water.

- Remove the gibbets from the duck and discard. Trim any skin at the neck and remove excess fat from around the main cavity and remove wing tips. Wash the duck under cold water and dry with paper towels. Prick the skin all over with the tip of a knife. Season the duck inside and out with sea salt. Tuck onion, orange, and Rosemary into the cavity. Tie the legs together with butcher string

- Once the smoker has reached 225-250F, place your duck on the grates, breast side down. Cook the duck until the internal breast temperature reaches 165F (about four hours).

Prepare Acorn Squash:

- Preheat oven to 375F.

- Cut squash crosswise in half. Scoop out and discard seeds.

- Place squash halves cut sides down with butter in 13x9 baking dish. Bake uncovered 45 to 55 minutes or until fork tender

Prepare Melted Leeks:

- Cut the roots and the dark greens off. Remove the outer layer. Slice the remaining leek lengthwise, gently fan the leek out under running water and rinse any dirty away.

- In a 10" pan, heat the butter and olive oil over medium heat. Once the butter starts to foam, add the leeks, 1/2 teaspoon of salt and stir. Adjust the heat to medium-low and cover with a lid. Cook for about 25 minutes.

- Remove the leeks from the heat and cool.

To serve:

- Fill roasted acorn squash with smoked duck, melted leeks, sunny side up duck egg. Bake at 325F for 15 minutes. Finish with truffle salt.

eat this with...
Adelaida Pinot Noir

roasted bone marrow by FARMstead ED

Warm marrow served on toast with lemon dressed parsley is a rustic appetizer. FARMstead ED recommends sourcing ingredients from these local producers: Templeton Hills Beef, Windrose Farm, The Groves on 41, Talley Farms and Spice of Life.

Yield 6 servings

12 two inch pieces beef middle-marrow bone
1 bunch Italian parsley leaves, chopped
Coarse ground sea salt, to taste
1 ½ tablespoons fresh lemon juice
5 tablespoons extra-virgin olive oil
2 shallots, very thinly sliced
Salt and pepper, to taste
Toasted white bread points

eat this with...
Adelaida HMR Pinot Noir
Brecon Estate Cabernet Franc
Caliza Syrah
Cass Mourvèdre
Castoro Cabernet Sauvignon
Graveyard Tombstone Red
Penman Springs Meritage
Seven Oxen Cassidy
Tablas Creek Mourvèdre
Windward Pinot Noir

- Preheat the oven to 350F.

- Put bones in an ovenproof pan and season with coarse ground sea salt and 1/2 of chopped parsley. Roast until marrow is loose and soft but not melted, about 20 minutes.

- Whisk together lemon juice and oil in medium bowl. Stir in shallots. Season with salt and pepper to taste. Toss in remaining parsley just prior to serving.

- Arrange the bones on a platter family style and pass the toast and sea salt. To eat, loosen the marrow with small forks or knives, spread on toast and top with a pinch of sea salt and some of the parsley salad.

lamb sliders by Annie Browne, Hoot 'n Annie

*These tasty little burgers are a huge hit when you have friends over for a BBQ.
The cherry chutney and goat cheese elevate the lamb flavors.*

Yield 8 sliders

1 pound ground lamb
4 cloves of garlic, chopped fine
2 sprigs fresh Rosemary, chopped fine
½ cup crumbled goat cheese
Salt and fresh ground pepper to taste
1/2 cup soft goat cheese, sliced
8 slider buns, toasted
Fresh basil, chopped

Cherry Chutney

1 cup dried cherries
1/4 cup red wine
2 tablespoons olive oil
1 chopped onion

- For the chutney: Place the cherries in a small bowl and cover with red wine to soak. Heat a skillet over medium heat, add olive oil. Sauté the onions until they start to caramelize, then add the dried cherries and wine. Cook over low heat for 10 minutes.

- For the patties: Combine lamb, garlic, Rosemary, cheese crumbles and season with salt and pepper. Form into slider-sized patties. Cook on a hot grill. Halfway through grilling flip the patties and add the sliced goat cheese. Approximately 3-4 minutes per side for medium/medium rare.

- Serve on toasted buns with cherry chutney and basil.

eat this with...

Brecon Estate Cabernet Franc
Cass Mourvèdre
Graveyard Tombstone Red
P.S. Cellars Grenache/Syrah
Penman Springs Petite Sirah
San Marcos Creek Cabernet Franc
Seven Oxen Tannat
Tablas Creek Syrah
Windward Pinot Noir

pork belly by Tablas Creek

Pomegranate glazed pork belly makes a delicious appetizer. The chef recommends serving this with roasted shiitake mushrooms and celeriac puree. The belly itself is good just sliced all on its own.

Serves 6

2 pounds pork belly, in slab form
Kosher salt and pepper, to taste

Pomegranate Glaze:

16 ounces pomegranate juice
1/2 cup sugar
1/4 teaspoon salt

> eat this with...
> Tablas Creek Counoise

- Take pork belly out of the refrigerator and leave out for at least 30 minutes. While the meat is coming to room temperature, preheat the oven to 350F. Line a rimmed baking sheet with aluminium foil. Dry the skin of the pork belly thoroughly before seasoning generously with salt and pepper. Place on baking sheet and bake for approximately 1 1/2 hours.

- While the pork belly is in the oven, prepare the glaze. In a small saucepan, whisk together the pomegranate juice, sugar and salt. Bring to a boil, then reduce the heat to a steady slow boil. The sauce should reduce to a syrup-like consistency (approximately 15 minutes).

- During the last 1/2 hour of cooking the pork belly use a pastry brush to brush on a thin layer of the glaze to the top of the belly every 10 minutes. Try to keep the glaze centered on the skin, if excess glaze pools on the bottom of the pan, it could burn easily and leave your pork belly excessively caramelized.

- When pork belly is finished cooking, allow it to rest on a cutting board for 15 minutes before serving. Slice into 3 inch pieces and finish with remaining pomegranate glaze.

wild boar bacon tart by Ryan Swarthout, Paso Robles Inn Steakhouse

These tarts are a favorite at Graveyard Vineyards' winemaker dinners. You make these as one large tart, or individual, serving sized tarts for an attractive presentation.

Yield 6 servings

1 refrigerated rolled pie crust (from a 15 ounce package)
4 slices wild boar bacon, cut crosswise into 1/4-inch slices
6 cups baby spinach
1 1/2 pounds yellow onions (about 4), halved and cut crosswise into 1/4 inch slices
3/4 teaspoon salt
1/4 teaspoon dried thyme
3/4 cup heavy cream
1/4 teaspoon black pepper
1/4 cup shredded Gruyere cheese

> **eat this with...**
> Graveyard Vineyards Chardonnay

- Heat oven to 375F.

- Fit pie crust into 9 inch tart pan. Trim excess crust from top edge of tart pan. Bake for 15 minutes weighted with dry bean and parchment paper. Remove from oven and allow to cool.

- Heat a large nonstick skillet over medium heat. Add bacon to skillet and cook, stirring often, for 8 minutes. Add spinach to skillet and cook 1 minute, stirring until wilted. Using a slotted spoon, remove bacon mixture to a paper-towel-lined plate.

- Add onions, 1/4 teaspoon salt and the thyme. Cover and cook 25 minutes over medium heat, stirring occasionally, or until browned. Add bacon mixture and stir to combine. Add heavy cream and black pepper. Cook until mixture is thick.

- Spoon filling into tart shell and top with Gruyere cheese. Optional: garnish with sliced green onions. Serve immediately.

chapter 3 - salads

sunshine kale & quinoa salad by Lori Foster, Spice of Life

Eat The Rainbow! Your body will shine inside and out with this delicious and healthy salad. A perfect salad to make ahead or serve immediately. You can prep and mix the first 5 ingredients ahead of time and store in airtight container in refrigerator for up to 4-5 days.

Yield 4-6 servings

1 cup quinoa, rinsed
1 bunch Italian kale, cut into small pieces
2-3 carrots, peeled, cut into small pieces
1-2 red bell peppers, cut into small pieces
¼-½ head red cabbage, cut into small pieces
1 handful fresh parsley, chopped
1 avocado, sliced
1 - 2 tablespoons fresh lemon juice
Pea sprouts
3-4 tablespoons Feta cheese
4-5 tablespoons candied pecans, chopped

"Greek Influence" Balsamic Dressing:

1 cup olive oil
¼ cup white balsamic
2 tablespoons rice vinegar
1 tablespoon fig balsamic vinegar
2 tablespoons Spice of Life "Greek Influence" spice blend

- Add quinoa and 2 cups water to a medium size pot over medium-high heat. Cover and bring to a boil. Reduce heat and simmer, covered, for 20 minutes or until water is absorbed. Remove from heat and let sit for 10 minutes. Uncover, fluff with fork and transfer to a large bowl to completely cool.

- In large bowl add kale, carrots, red bell peppers, red cabbage, parsley and lightly toss. Add quinoa and toss.

- Add desired amount of "Greek Influence" balsamic dressing and toss to completely coat.

- Drizzle fresh lemon juice over salad. Either serve on individual plates and top with avocado, nuts, goat cheese, and sprouts or toss all together and serve in large bowl.

eat this with...
Graveyard Ascender
Penman Springs Dry Humor
Riverstar Riesling

baby greens & persimmon salad by FARMstead ED

Fresh, bright persimmons are the star in this Baby Greens, Persimmon and Toasted Walnut Salad with *Lemon Honey Vinaigrette* & *Fresh Goat Cheese*. FARMstead ED recommends sourcing ingredients from these local producers and purveyors: Talley Farms, Windrose Farm, Stepladder Creamery, The Groves on 41, Wine Diva Jams, and Spice of Life

Yield 6 servings

2 medium ripe Fuyu persimmons
1/3 cup walnuts, shelled and toasted
1/4 cup goat cheese crumbles
6 packed cups baby greens

Lemon Honey Vinaigrette

1/4 cup fresh lemon juice (about 2 small lemons)
1 tablespoon minced shallots
1 teaspoon Dijon mustard
1 tablespoon honey
1/2 cup lemon olive oil
Pinch of kosher salt
Finely grated zest of 2 small lemons

- **To make the vinaigrette:** Whisk lemon juice, shallots, mustard, salt, lemon zest and honey together. Drizzle the oil into the juice mixture in a slow, steady stream while whisking rapidly and constantly until the vinaigrette thickens slightly. Serve immediately or refrigerate in an airtight container for up to 3 days until ready to use. Whisk again to re-emulsify the vinaigrette before using.

- **For the salad:** Use a sharp paring knife or veggie peeler to cut skins off the persimmons, then slice the fruit into very thin rounds (if you have a mandolin, use it set at 1/8 inch). Line a large platter with the slices. Toss the greens with enough vinaigrette to lightly coat and pile the mixture on top of the persimmons. Top with toasted walnuts and goat cheese crumbles. Drizzle with the a little more vinaigrette and serve.

eat this with...
AmByth Estate Viognier

waldorf salad by Lisa Pretty

This classic salad is one that people continue to enjoy, year after year. Although you can use any mix of lettuce that you like, I find the texture of bib lettuce really works well with the other salad ingredients.

Yield 4 servings

1/2 cup non-fat Greek yogurt
2 tablespoons minced fresh flat-leaf parsley
1 teaspoon honey
Zest from 1/2 lemon, finely grated
Freshly ground black pepper

2 large crisp apples or pears, cored and diced
2 ribs celery, chopped
6 cups bib lettuce, washed and torn
1/2 lemon, juiced
1/2 cup toasted walnuts halves
1/4 cup blue cheese crumbles

- Whisk the yogurt, parsley, honey, and lemon zest in a large bowl and season generously with pepper.

- Add the apples (or pears), celery and lettuce to the bowl, and sprinkle with the lemon juice; then toss with the dressing from the bottom of the bowl.

- Divide the salad among 4 salad plates and top with walnuts and blue cheese.

eat this with...

Adelaida Anna's White
Brecon Estate Albariño
Graveyard Tombstone White
Locatelli Chardonnay
P.S. Cellars Arneis
Pear Valley Chardonnay
Penman Springs Dry Humour
San Marcos Creek White Merlot

dad's caesar salad by Joseph Glunz, Gluntz Family Winery

The secret ingredient that makes this so good is the croutons. The anchovy paste is also a star ingredient; however you may need to skip telling some people that!

Yield 6 servings
- 2 tablespoons butter
- 1 split top bread loaf, cut in 3/4 inch cubes
- 3 cloves garlic, minced
- 1 large head Romaine lettuce, rinsed and chopped

Dressing:
- 3/4 cup olive oil
- 2 teaspoons fresh ground black pepper
- 4 medium sized garlic cloves, minced
- 3/4 teaspoon dry mustard
- 1 1/2 cups grated Parmesan cheese
- 1 teaspoon Worcestershire sauce
- 1 extra large pasteurized egg
- 1/2 cup fresh lemon juice
- 1/2 teaspoon salt
- Anchovy paste, to taste

eat this with...
Glunz Family Winery Viognier

- Pre-heat oven to 325F.

- Croutons: These are a pain to make, so you may want to consider making extra and freezing them. Place the cut bread on a sided cookie sheet. Place sheet in the oven and bake for approximately 15 minutes, stirring every 5 minutes. The goal is to dry the bread. They should be a golden brown when done. Remove from oven and set aside.

- In a small sauce pan, melt the butter and add 3 cloves of minced garlic. Remove from heat and let the garlic steep in the butter while you make the dressing.

- Dressing: Whisk all the dressing ingredient well. Cover and refrigerate until ready to use. Note: if you do not have pasteurized eggs, you will need to coddle the eggs. To Coddle: boil water in sauce pan then add the egg for 1 minute and remove to cold water. Crack the egg open and spoon out any white attached to the shells.

- Back to the croutons:. Place the croutons in a frying pan over medium low heat, drizzle with the garlic butter. Try to get some of the garlic butter on all the croutons. If it looks dry, add a little olive oil. Heating them for 15 minutes will help toast them a bit more and help spread the garlic butter. Stir frequently during this time.

- Put the chilled lettuce in a large salad bowl, then spoon on the dressing and mix going down the sides to the bottom and up. Take care not to bruise the lettuce. Add more dressing and repeat the mixing process until you feel the lettuce is coated but not soaked.

- Add the croutons and serve. Offer guests a pepper grinder as they may like extra pepper.

grilled caesar salad by The HATCH

Romaine lettuce is perfect for the grill. This is a quick Caesar recipe and if you really want to save time you can just use store bought croutons.

Yield 4 servings
- **4 hearts Romaine, split lengthwise**
- **Olive oil**
- **Kosher salt**
- **Croutons (see page 77 for homemade)**

Dressing:
- **1 egg yolk**
- **½ tablespoon whole grain mustard**
- **3 tablespoons minced garlic**
- **1 cup olive oil**
- **1/8 cup champagne vinegar**
- **Salt & Pepper, to taste**
- **1 cup Parmesan, grated with microplane**

- For Dressing: Whisk together egg yolk, mustard and garlic. Continue whisking while adding oil in a slow, steady stream. Once incorporated, add vinegar in a slow, steady stream, then add salt and pepper to taste.

- Rub cut side of romaine hearts with oil and sprinkle with kosher salt. Grill over medium high heat until lightly colored and charred in some places, 1-2 minutes. Chop hearts into bite-sized pieces, add croutons, toss with dressing to taste and pile on plates. Shower with grated Parmesan.

eat this with...
Riverstar Tempranillo

eat this with...
P.S. Cellars Barbera

beet salad by Chef Thomas Drahos, Blue Heron

This Italian inspired recipe of roasted tri color beet salad, basil balsamic, goat cheese mousse, and crispy beet chips is a wonderful salad to make when you have fresh beets.

Yield 8 servings

1 bunch each of yellow, purple and pink beets (cleaned and tops removed)
About a handful beet greens reserved
1 pound goat cheese softened at room temperature
1 bunch of basil
1 tablespoon honey
1/2 cup balsamic
2 clove of garlic
1 shallot peeled
1 tablespoon whole grain mustard
2 cups of extra virgin olive oil
1 cup red wine vinegar
Oil for frying

- Preheat the oven to 350F.

- Place beets in separate heat proof dishes. Divide the red wine vinegar between each pan, evenly cover the beets with water, and then tightly with a lid or foil. Bake until beets become tender about three hours or so checking to make sure the liquid levels are good throughout. Chill and remove the outer skin, then cut into desired shapes and sizes. Reserve for plating.

- Crush one clove of garlic and mix into the softened goat cheese. Reserve for plating.

- In the blender put the balsamic vinegar, mustard, honey, garlic, shallot, and basil. Turn the blender on medium high speed and slowly drizzle in the olive oil until the liquid becomes thick, emulsified and coats the back of the spoon. Reserve for plating.

- Using a twelve inch round plate, spoon the goat cheese mousse in several spots evenly around the plate, next alternate beet color red, yellow, pink then repeat across the plate. Top with beet greens. Next spoon on some of the basil balsamic dressing.

warm spinach salad by Annie Browne, Hoot n' Annie

The apples really are the star of this dish. But who doesn't love toasted nuts and pomegranate seeds on warm spinach?

Yield 4-6 servings
2 tablespoon butter
1 apple, cored and sliced
2 tablespoon olive oil
2 tablespoon balsamic vinegar
1 bag of baby spinach leaves
Salt, to taste
¼ cup pomegranate seeds
1/3 cup chopped hazelnuts, roasted

- Heat the butter over medium heat in a skillet. Add the apple slices and let them brown in the butter, about 4 minutes on each side. Remove the apples and drain on paper towels.

- Add the olive oil and vinegar to the pan and warm just until blended. Add the spinach, season with salt and toss it quickly. Remove the spinach and place in a serving dish.

- Top with apple, pomegranate seeds, and hazelnuts.

crab & avocado salad by Tablas Creek

This crab and avocado salad with a Meyer lemon vinaigrette is the perfect start to any dinner, or impress your friends by serving this as a light lunch.

eat this with...
Tablas Creek Côtes De Tablas Blanc

Yield serves 8

>   2 pounds live Dungeness crab (1 crab)
>   1 tablespoon mayonnaise
>   Juice of 1/2 Meyer lemon
>   2 avocados
>   Salt & pepper to taste

Vinaigrette

>   1 1/2 Meyer lemons, zested and juiced
>   1/2 Ruby Red grapefruit, juiced
>   1 tablespoon honey
>   1/4 cup grape seed (or any neutral) oil
>   Heavy cream (optional)
>   Salt & pepper to taste

- Bring stock pot of water to a boil. Immerse crab and cover pot, leaving a gap for steam to escape. Boil for 12-15 minutes. Remove from boiling water and cool. Remove meat and set aside in bowl. Once the crab cools, mix crab with 1/2 tablespoon mayonnaise. Add more to your liking. Fold in lemon juice and salt and pepper. Set in refrigerator until ready to use.

- In a small bowl, whisk lemon juice, zest, grapefruit juice, honey, salt and pepper until combined. While whisking constantly, slowly steam in oil to emulsify. For a creamy dressing: in a separate bowl, beat heavy cream to form soft peaks. Fold in 1/2 a tablespoon at a time into the dressing, until it reaches the desired consistency.

- Quarter and peel avocados, then season with salt and pepper. Place a generous tablespoon of crab salad on top. Drizzle vinaigrette (about 1 teaspoon) on top of crab and avocado.

- Garnish with microgreens and a dash of olive oil, if desired.

ahi crudo salad by Amy Butler, Ranchero Cellars

When sashimi-grade ahi tuna is available, this ahi crudo salad with hazelnut gremolata is the perfect recipe to serve as a lunch entree or salad as a delicious start to dinner.

Yield 6 servings
- 2 cups baby arugula
- ½ fennel bulb, thinly sliced
- 6 tablespoons olive oil
- 2 tablespoons rice vinegar

- 12 ounces fresh sashimi-grade ahi tuna, sliced thinly across the grain

For Gremolata:
- 1/3 cup chopped hazelnuts, toasted
- 1 tablespoon lemon zest
- 1/3 cup chopped Italian parsley
- 2 garlic cloves, smashed
- 1/3 cup olive oil
- Salt and pepper, to taste

- **Make Gremolata:** In a food processor or mortar and pestle, combine dry ingredients. Mash or chop to a fine paste. Drizzle in olive oil and season with salt and pepper to taste. Stir well before using.

- **Assemble salad:** Lightly dress arugula and fennel with oil and vinegar. Arrange on a serving plate and top with sliced ahi. Drizzle ahi slices generously with gremolata. Garnish with chopped fennel fronds if desired

eat this with...
Ranchero Cellars Chrome

brussels sprout salad by Ange Payton, Drink with Experts

This Shaved Brussels Sprout Salad with Warm Double Bacon & Beer Vinaigrette is the perfect winter salad to serve as a side dish or as a salad course on its own.

Yield 6 servings
- 2 pounds Brussels sprouts, shaved
- 6 slices of bacon, cooked and crumbled
- ¾ cup of dried cranberries
- 1 cup chopped pecans
- 1-2 green apples, peeled and diced, medium
- Salt & pepper, to taste

Vinaigrette:
- 4 ounces pancetta, cooked and crumbled
- 2 tablespoons reserved bacon fat
- 1-2 teaspoons Dijon mustard
- 3 tablespoons maple syrup
- 2 tablespoons apple cider vinegar
- 2 tablespoons hoppy red ale
- 1-4 tablespoons extra virgin olive oil, as needed
- Salt & pepper, to taste

- ❧ Carefully cut the Brussels sprouts into very thin slices using a mandolin or a very sharp knife. Place shaved sprouts into a large bowl and toss to separate layers. Add bacon, cranberries and green apples. Toss to mix.

- ❧ In a sauté pan, add the pecans over medium heat and toss around to toast, about 2-5 minutes, then add to salad.

- ❧ Make the Vinaigrette: In a small heat proof bowl, whisk together the Dijon mustard, maple syrup, apple cider vinegar, beer.

- ❧ In medium sauté pan, heat the reserved bacon fat and cook the pancetta. Use a slotted spoon to scoop the pancetta out of the pan and whisk into vinaigrette. Pour the hot bacon fat into the vinaigrette and whisk. Add 1 to 2 tablespoons of olive oil if the vinaigrette is too thin. Pour the warm vinaigrette over the salad and toss to coat. Serve immediately.

eat this with...
Red October, a hoppy red ale

venison carpaccio by Richard Verhagen, Hurricane Kitchen

Be sure to ask your butcher for a boneless venison steak or loin. Explain that you are making carpaccio (very important). Chef Richard recommends J&R Natural Meats for a local source.

Yield 4-6 servings

1 pound boneless venison steak or loin
Mixed organic greens
White onions
Tomatillos
Fresh spinach
Fresh basil
Fresh mint
Roma tomatoes
Sugar snap peas
Raspberries
Balsamic vinaigrette
Montreal steak spice
Olive oil
Caraway seed
Cane sugar
Bleu cheese

eat this with...

Barrelhouse Brewing Mango IPA
Cass Rockin' One
Donati Family Winery Petit Verdot
Four Lanterns Grenache/Syrah
Graveyard Tombstone Red
MCV Wines Pink
P.S. Cellars Grenache/Syrah
Penman Springs Petit Verdot
Tablas Creek Patelin de Tablas

- Marinate venison in olive oil and Montreal steak spice, and refrigerate for one day. Use 1 heaping teaspoon of Montreal steak spice per pound of venison.

- Prior to serving, freeze venison for about one hour. This will solidify the meat and aide in creating paper thin slices.

- Raspberry Vinaigrette: Add 2 cups of raspberries, 1/2 cup of balsamic vinaigrette, 1/2 cup of olive oil, and 1/2 cup of cane sugar to a mixing bowl. Add 1 tablespoon of caraway seed and mix well using a hand blender. Refrigerate for one hour.

- Salad: Rustically chop 2 small white onions, 6-8 tomatillos, and 5-6 Roma tomatoes. Add to a salad bowl or large mixing bowl with mixed greens, sugar snap peas, basil, spinach, and mint.

- Remove venison from the freezer, and using a meat slicer, mandolin, or fillet knife, slice venison into paper thin pieces.

- Add the raspberry vinaigrette to the salad bowl and toss liberally. Transfer the contents of the salad bowl on to serving plates. Add venison to the salad on the serving plates. Add crumbled Bleu cheese. Sprinkle lightly with Montreal steak spice and serve.

chapter 4 - soups & stews

eat this with...
Adelaida Syrah
Cass Grenache
P.S. Cellars Barbera
Riverstar Tempranillo
Seven Oxen Zinfandel

kabocha squash soup by Chef Benjamin Harrison

Chef Ben's vegan Kabocha squash soup is finished with a homemade pesto oil. Source local, fresh ingredients when making this recipe.

Yield 6 servings
- 5 cloves garlic
- 8 ounces ginger root
- 1 ½ cups olive oil
- 6 medium carrots peeled (reserve 1 cup of tops)
- 8 pounds Kabocha squash

- 32 ounces Thai coconut milk
- 12 basil leaves
- 15 mint leaves chocolate or grapefruit
- 1 tablespoon ground cardamom
- 1 tablespoon garam marsala
- Salt to taste

- Preheat oven to 375F.

- Peel and remove seeds from Kabocha squash and chop into one inch pieces. Place in bowl. Add ¼ cup olive oil, 3 heavy pinches of salt, stir and place onto a sheet pan. Cook in oven for 20 minutes.

- Chop garlic, ginger, and carrots; place in soup pot, add ¼ cup olive oil, bring to medium heat, stir frequently for 4 minutes. On a separate burner heat vegetable stock. Add roasted squash to the soup pot along with the coconut milk. Decrease soup stove burner to low and add simmering vegetable stock. Stirring occasionally, incorporate all ingredients while keeping them from sticking to the bottom of the pot. If contents do stick, don't scrape it from the bottom. Allow soup to simmer for about 15 minutes, then turn off heat and add spices, and half of the basil and mint leaves. With an immersion blender, blend all the contents of the soup.

- For pesto oil, start a blanching liquid with 4 cups water and 2 tablespoons salt, bring to a boil then turn off. Add remaining basil, mint and 1 cup of tender tops of carrots. Leave in water for only 15 seconds.

- Prepare an ice bath in a large bowl. Pour blanching liquid through a fine metal sieve and dunk the greens into the ice bath. Lightly squeeze the greens and place in a blender. Add a cup of olive oil and blend all until completely emulsified.

- Serve soup drizzled with the pesto oil.

cioppino by Bruce Finch, A Party For Your Palate

Bruce's Cioppino recipe has a lot of ingredients; however, once you taste the broth, you will understand why! Loaded with shellfish, this is a seafood lovers dream dish. Bruce won both Judges' and People's Choice Award for his Cioppino at Paso's Cioppino & Vino event – I am so happy he agreed to share this recipe.

Yield 6-8 servings

3 tablespoons butter
1 large white onion, diced
8 green onions, chopped
4 stalks celery, small dice
2 fennel bulbs, small dice
1 red bell pepper, small dice
2 yellow bell pepper, small dice
4 large cloves garlic, minced
1 bunch parsley, minced
1 teaspoon red pepper flakes
60 ounces tomato sauce
6 ounces tomato paste
4 tomatoes seeded and diced
5 cups chardonnay, divided
16 ounces clam juice
8 basil leaves, very thinly sliced
4 bay leaves
2 teaspoons dried oregano
2 teaspoons dried thyme

1 ½ pounds white fish, cut into bite size pieces
1 ½ pounds bay scallops, rinsed
20 41-50 raw prawns, peeled and de-veined, tails removed
20 41-50 raw prawns, peeled and de-veined, tails removed, minced
1 pound clam meat, minced
18 clams, scrubbed and cleaned
18 mussels, scrubbed and de-bearded
1 pound calamari (tubes and tentacles preferred)
2 whole crabs, cooked, cleaned and cracked, legs only, belly meat harvested, set aside and reserved
Lemons and fennel fronds to garnish
Salt and pepper, to taste

Chef's note: *You can use any white fish that you like. - snapper, cod, Mahi Mahi, and halibut all work great.*

eat this with...
Adelaida HMR Pinot Noir
Bushong Albariño
Brecon Albariño
Graveyard Tombstone Pink
JUSTIN Viognier
P.S. Cellars Barbera
Penman Springs Rosé
Riverstar Riesling

- In a large pot, add butter and melt over medium high heat. Add in both onions and stir until onions just turns clear. Add in celery, bell peppers, diced fennel, and red pepper flakes and continue to stir until vegetables become just al dente. Do not brown vegetables. Add in garlic and stir another minute or two.

- Add in tomatoes, sauce, paste, 4 cups wine, clam juice, oregano, thyme and bay leaves. Stir to incorporate tomato paste. Reduce heat to medium low and simmer for about 1 – 1 1/2 hours.

- 30 minutes before serving, add in remaining wine, parsley, basil, white fish, minced prawns and clam meat, crab belly meat and crab. Bring cioppino to a simmer. Season to taste. 10 minutes before service, add in prawns, clams and mussels. Cook until prawns turn orange and clams and mussels open (discard any that don't open). Add in scallops and calamari. Stir for 2 minutes.

- Remove bay leaves and serve with warm French bread or garlic bread for dipping, and lemon wedges on the side.

roasted potato soup by Ange Payton, Drink with Experts

This cheesy roasted potato soup will be a huge hit with anyone who enjoys a fully loaded baked potato. Serve the garnish on the side and let your guests play.

Yield 6 servings
- 1/2 cup softened butter (1 stick)
- 1/4 cup extra-virgin olive oil
- 2 tablespoons chopped green onion
- Salt & Pepper, to taste
- 3 Red Small Red, large dice
- 3 Yukon Gold Potatoes, large dice

- 1/2 medium onion, diced fine
- 1 tablespoon olive oil
- 3 tablespoons butter
- 3 tablespoons flour
- 1 cup heavy cream
- 1/3 cup sour cream
- 2 cups stock (chicken or vegetable)
- 2 cups Gruyere/Swiss cheese blend, grated
- Garnish (optional): bacon crumbs, green onions, shredded Gruyere

- Preheat oven to 450F

- Make the Butter: In small bowl, mix together green onions, olive oil, salt and pepper, and 1/2 cup butter.

- Roast the Potatoes: Dice the red and Yukon Gold potatoes. Place the diced potatoes into the bowl with the butter mixture and toss to coat. Spread evenly on a large baking sheet. Place in oven and roast for 20-30 minutes, until done.

eat this with...
Majestic Surf, a West Coast IPA

- Make the Soup: Melt butter in a medium sized pot. Add olive oil and onion then sauté until translucent. Sprinkle in flour and sauté at least 2-3 minutes. Add cream and sour cream, stirring frequently until it begins to thicken. Add stock and cook 15 minutes. Add cheese and cook for 10-15 minutes longer or until cheese has fully melted. Season with salt and pepper.

- Serve: Ladle the soup, 2/3rds full into bowls. Carefully place a stack of roasted potatoes into the center of each bowl. Garnish with any or all of the optional toppings.

chickpea & spinach stew by Lisa Pretty

This Spanish inspired stew is very fragrant and makes a nice vegetarian lunch in the winter.

Yield 4 servings
- 6 peeled garlic cloves
- 1/4 cup olive oil
- 1 thick slice white country bread
- 2 tablespoons paprika
- 1 pinch saffron
- 2 tablespoons sherry vinegar
- 4 cups canned chickpeas, rinsed
- 1 cup tomato sauce
- 1 teaspoon ground cumin
- 1/2 pound spinach, washed
- Salt & pepper, to taste

eat this with...
Pear Valley Aglianico
P.S. Cellars Grenache/Syrah
San Marcos Creek Nebbiolo
Seven Oxen Cassidy
Ranchita Canyon Vineyard Sangiovese

- Sauté garlic in olive oil in a small skillet over medium-low heat. Remove garlic when lightly browned and set aside.

- Toast bread in the skillet about 1 minute on each side on medium heat. Remove bread and add paprika, saffron and vinegar.

- Pound garlic & bread in a mortar or bowl to make a thick paste.

- Place chickpeas, tomato sauce and cumin in a large saucepan. Bring to low boil and simmer for 30 minutes. Add spinach and simmer for 5 minutes. Add paprika/saffron mixture and garlic/bread paste to chickpeas and simmer approximately 5 minutes. Season with salt & pepper.

split pea soup by Lisa Pretty

While it is possible to make a vegetarian split pea soup, it just isn't the same without the ham bone! I like mine pea soup super thick.

Yield 6 servings

2 1/4 cups dried split peas, sorted and rinsed
8 cups water
1 large onion, chopped
1 teaspoon celery seeds
1 teaspoon pepper
1 ham bone or 2 pounds
1 medium carrot, fine dice
Salt, to taste

- Bring water to a boil in 4-quart Dutch oven. Add peas and boil uncovered 5 minutes; remove from heat. Cover and let stand 1 hour.

- Return Dutch oven to heat, stir in onion, celery and pepper. Add ham bone. Heat to boiling; reduce heat. Cover and simmer about 1 hour 30 minutes or until peas are tender.

- Remove ham bone; remove ham from bone. Trim excess fat from ham; cut ham into 1/2-inch pieces. Stir ham and carrots into soup. Heat to boiling; reduce heat to simmer. Cover and simmer about 30 minutes or until carrots are tender and soup is desired consistency.

eat this with...
Cass Marsanne
Penman Springs Dry Humour
Ranchero Cellars Chrome
Riverstar Riesling
Tackitt Family Gewurztraminer

chicken and dumplings by Lisa Pretty

*I don't know what it is about chicken and dumplings. It is one of my favorite dishes.
I don't go for the perfectly shaped dumpling, for me it is more about the flavor.
Comfort food at its finest!*

Yield 4 servings

- 2 tablespoons olive oil
- 1 medium onion, chopped
- 2 carrots, peeled and sliced
- 4 chicken thighs, cooked and chopped
- 4 cups chicken broth (preferably homemade)
- 1 teaspoon celery salt
- 1 tablespoon fresh chopped parsley
- 2 bay leaves
- Salt and pepper, to taste

For the Dumplings:

- 2 cups all-purpose flour
- 1 tablespoon baking powder
- 1/2 teaspoon salt
- 2 large egg, beaten
- 3/4 cup buttermilk
- 1 tablespoon fresh chopped parsley

- Heat the olive oil in a medium stock pot over medium heat. Sauté the onion and carrots. Add chicken, broth, celery salt, parsley and bay leaves. Bring to a boil and then reduce heat to simmer for 30 minutes.

- Make dumplings: Sift dry ingredients together in a large bowl. In a small bowl, beat the eggs and milk together. Stir in parsley. Pour the liquid into the dry ingredients and gently fold. Mix until the dough comes together, it should be thick and cake-like.

- Remove the bay leaves and season the soup with salt and pepper. Drop large spoonfuls of dumpling dough into the soup. They should not crowd or touch each other. Cover the pot and let the dumplings poach for 10- 15 minutes until they are firm and puffy.

eat this with...

Adelaida Anna's White
Brecon Estate Albariño
Cass Rousanne
Glunz Family Winery Viognier
Graveyard Chardonnay
Locatelli Chardonnay
Pear Valley Tom's Oak Chardonnay
San Marcos Creek Chardonnay
Tablas Creek Viognier

beef broth by Darian Buckles, Templeton Hills Beef

Darian adapted this roasted broth recipe from Lynne Curry's cookbook "Pure Beef". Once you make your own beef broth you will not want to go back to store bought ever again! It makes a soothing cup of broth or used as a base for soups, stews, or noodles.

Yield 4-6 quarts

6-7 pounds bones, including some meaty bones
2 tablespoons olive oil
1 teaspoon kosher salt
2 large onions chopped
2 large carrots chopped
2 celery stalks, chopped
1 head garlic, papery skin removed and top 1/3 cut off to expose the cloves
1 teaspoon cracked black peppercorns
1/4 teaspoon dried thyme
2 dried bay leaves

eat this with...

Adelaida Anna's Red
Brecon Estate Cabernet Franc
Cass Rockin' One Red
Graveyard Cabernet Sauvignon
Glunz Family Winery Zinfandel
Ranchero Cellars Revolver
Riverstar Sunset Red
San Marcos Creek Merlot
Seven Oxen Cassidy

- Pre-heat the oven to 425F. Rub olive oil over bones and sprinkle them with kosher salt. Arrange them in a single layer on a large roasting pan or rimmed baking sheet. Roast bones for 30 minutes. Turn the bones and add all the vegetables, except garlic to pan. Return to the oven and continue roasting for 20 minutes.

- Remove roasting pan from the oven and reduce oven temperature to 200F. Use tongs to transfer bones into your largest stock pot. Scoop in the vegetables using a slotted spoon. Pour in 4 quarts cool water. Add two cups of water to the roasting pan, scraping up the brown bits, then add all of this liquid to the stock pot. Add garlic, peppercorns, thyme and bay leaves as well. Put pot in the oven and cook, uncovered at 200F overnight. In the morning remove stock pot from oven and allow to cool to room temperature. This can be accomplished quickly by placing the stock pot in a sink filled with cold water. Then refrigerate for at least 6 hours.

- Once cold, remove any fat from the surface. Use a colander and cheesecloth or a fine towel to strain broth. Once cool, the broth will be gelatinous and you will need to rewarm it until it becomes pourable. Store stock in 1-2 quart containers for 1 week in the refrigerator or up to 6 months in the freezer.

bacon and lentil soup by Chef Jacob, Cass Café

Your house will smell amazing when you make this soup!

Yield 6 servings
  1 cup brown or green lentils
  5 slices high quality, thick cut bacon
  1 sweet onion, finely diced
  1 leek, dark green portion removed, finely diced, rinsed and drained
  1 carrot, finely diced
  2 celery ribs, finely diced
  2 bay leaves
  6+ cups homemade chicken stock, or low-sodium broth
  2 tablespoons Italian parsley, chopped
  Kosher salt and black pepper, to taste

eat this with...
Cass Rockin' One Red

- Rinse the lentils well under cold water, then drain and set aside.

- In a medium stock pot, add the bacon and cook until crispy and browned. Remove bacon and set aside to cool.

- Using the rendered bacon fat, sauté the onion leek, celery, carrot, and bay leaves for approximately 5 minutes. Add the lentils and chicken stock, and bring mixture to a boil. Lower the heat, and skim the surface of foam as needed. Simmer, partially covered, for about 40 minutes, until lentils are soft but not mushy.

- Chop up the bacon and return it to the soup, along with ½ of the chopped parsley. Simmer for a few minutes more, then remove the bay leaves and discard.

- Ladle into serving bowls and garnish with additional parsley.

eat this with...
LXV Tempranillo

mutton shorba by Neeta Mittal, LXV Wines

Shorba is an Arabic word that means soup. Mutton Shorba is an interesting soup,
made with bone-in mutton pieces, a perfect dish to be served at any party. It has an
absolutely delightful taste.

Yield 4 servings

2 tablespoons coconut oil	1 teaspoon turmeric powder
1 teaspoon cumin	3 teaspoons fennel seeds
1 cup chopped onion	3 bay leaves
1 tablespoon minced ginger	4 - 5 Slit green chillies
1 tablespoon minced garlic	1 cup coriander leaves with stem
1 pound goat meat	1 cup mint leaves
1/2 pound marrow bones	1 teaspoon red chili powder
1 inch cinnamon stick	Salt and pepper, to taste
5-6 green cardamom	
10 black peppercorns	

- In a large pan, add oil, cumin and onion. Fry over medium-high heat until soft, then add crushed ginger and garlic and fry until onion is light brown, add mutton, bones, all the spices in the left side ingredient list. Fry until the mutton is nicely seared.

- Add turmeric powder, fennel seeds, bay leaves, chopped coriander leaves and mint leaves, and slit green chilies, and cook for another 2-3 minutes. Then quickly stir fry the red chili powder in the oil for a few seconds until the oil absorbs the chili. Add 24 ounces of water and salt, cover the pan and cook until mutton is falling off the bones.

- When slightly cool remove mutton pieces, place in a bowl, and reserve for plating.

- Now using sieve, filter the shorba, squeeze out juices as much as possible, discard the rest. Taste and adjust the seasoning if required.

- In a soup bowl, place several mutton pieces at the centre and pour the shorba over it. Then drizzle few drops of garlic chili oil.

chapter 5 - entrées

pasta bake by Amy Butler, Ranchero Cellars

Amy's Pasta Bake with Meyer Lemons and Kale is the perfect dish for a lunch entree, a light supper or even a starter to a multi-course dinner. The flavors in this dish play in your mouth (in a good way!).

Yield 4-6 servings

> 3 tablespoons butter
> 3 tablespoons flour
> 1 cup whole milk, warmed
> ¼ cup dry white wine (Preferably Ranchero Cellars Chrome)
> 1 cup plus 2 tablespoons finely grated Parmesan or Pecorino cheese
> 4 cups Tuscan kale, ribs removed and coarsely chopped
> 1 pound bulk Italian sausage
> 1 Meyer lemon
> ½ pound pasta, any fun shape, cooked according to package directions, drained

eat this with...
Ranchero Cellars Chrome

- Brown and crumble the Italian sausage in a heavy skillet. Drain fat and set aside.

- Thinly slice the lemon and plunge slices into boiling water, blanching for 5-7 minutes. Drain carefully on towels, and cut half the slices into fine dice.

- Pre-heat oven to 375F.

- Make the Sauce: Place Butter in a heavy saucepan over medium-high heat. As soon as butter is melted, whisk in flour. Cook for 1 minute, then gradually whisk in warm milk, being careful not to form lumps. Bring mixture to a boil, stirring constantly. Reduce heat, add wine and chopped kale and simmer, about 1 minute.

- Assemble the Dish: Remove sauce from heat. Whisk in 1 cup cheese and stir in browned sausage, chopped lemon, and cooked pasta.

- Transfer to a buttered baking dish, top with remaining lemon slices, and cover with foil. Bake 25 minutes. Increase heat to 450F, uncover the dish, and sprinkle with remaining cheese. Bake until golden brown, 8-10 minutes.

mussels mariniere by Joseph Glunz, Glunz Family Winery

Joseph recommends using small Mussels, Prince Edward if available. Be sure to serve with plenty of bread to soak up all the wine sauce.

- Discard any broken or open mussels. Do not keep them in water or a sealed plastic bag as they will suffocate.

- In a large frying pan with lid, combine wine, shallots, thyme, garlic, cayenne pepper, and olive oil. Simmer, reducing liquid slightly. Increase heat to boil, then add the cream until liquid thickens.

- Add mussels, at high heat, stirring and coat them with the liquid. Cover for 30 -40 seconds and stir them again. Repeat this for a total of only 3 to 4 minutes. When mussels are open they are done.

- Taste sauce and adjust salt if necessary, then sprinkle with parsley. Discard any mussels that did not open.

- Serve in heated bowls and be sure to pour extra sauce over the top.

Yield 4 servings

4 pounds mussels, washed and de-bearded
1 cup dry white wine
1/4 cup finely chopped shallots
1/2 teaspoon dry thyme, crushed
2 garlic cloves, crushed
1 pinch cayenne pepper
1/4 cup olive oil
3/4 cup heavy cream
2 tablespoons fresh parsley, chopped fine
Salt if needed (the mussels will be salty)
Crusty baguette

eat this with...
Glunz Family Winery Zinfandel
Glunz Family Winery Viognier
Glunz Family Winery Chardonnay

sand dabs by Chico Mora, The Catch Seafood Bar and Grill

Chef Chico sources his sand dabs in Morro Bay. Topped with mushrooms in a wine sauce, this is a customer favorite in his restaurant. Serve with potato and seasonal vegetables.

Yield 4 servings
- **1 pound sand dabs**
- **Lemon**
- **Clarified butter**
- **Salt, to taste**

For mushroom sauce:
- **1 cup sliced mushrooms**
- **1 cup white wine**
- **4 teaspoons capers**
- **1 teaspoon dry dill**
- **Salt, to taste**

eat this with...
Penman Springs Dry Humour

- Sauté mushrooms in a tablespoon butter over medium high heat. Add the wine, capers, and dill and season with salt. Bring to a boil and then reduce heat. Allow sauce to simmer while you broil the sand dabs.

- Heat broiler. Place sand dabs on a baking sheet and squeeze lemon juice over the top, drizzle with clarified butter and season with salt. Broil for 90 seconds.

- Serve sand dabs, topped with mushroom sauce, with lemon wedges and extra clarified butter on the side.

mahi mahi Chico Mora, The Catch Seafood Bar and Grill

Mahi Mahi is a beautiful fish and only requires a few minutes to pan fry. Chef Chico serves his with clarified butter and lemons.

Yield 4 servings
  4 Mahi Mahi fillets
  3 tablespoons clarified butter
  Salt, to taste
  Lemon, cut into wedges

- Heat clarified butted in a large frying pan. Add mahi mahi and season with salt. Cook on high heat for 2 minutes per side.

- Serve with lemon wedges.

eat this with...
  Penman Springs Meritage

seared salmon by Johnny Jantz, Boccabella Farms

Chef Jantz created this seared salmon with asparagus recipe specifically to pair with Lazzare Sauvignon Blanc. The Boccabella Farms' olive oil is a key ingredient in both the salmon and the sauce.

Yield 4 servings
- 4 salmon fillets
- 1 tablespoon flour
- 1 teaspoon fresh lemon juice
- 2 tablespoons Boccabella extra virgin olive oil
- salt and pepper

For Asparagus:
- 1 bunch of asparagus, washed
- 1 tablespoon Boccabella extra virgin olive oil
- 1 teaspoon lemon zest
- Salt and pepper

For Citrus Butter Sauce:
- 1 cup Lazarre Sauvignon Blanc
- 5 tablespoons whole unsalted butter
- 1 tablespoon dill, chopped
- 1 tablespoon shallot, chopped
- 1 tablespoon fresh squeezed lemon juice
- 1 teaspoon lemon zest
- Salt and pepper, to taste

eat this with...
Lazzare Sauvignon Blanc

- For sauce: In a small saucepan, combine chopped shallot with Lazarre Sauvignon Blanc. On medium-low heat, reduce until you have a semi-thick syrup. Reduce heat to low, add lemon juice and slowly whisk in whole butter, a tablespoon at a time. Add fresh dill and lemon zest, season with salt and pepper.

- For salmon: Lightly season salmon fillets with salt and pepper, then sprinkle with flour. In a large sauté pan add Boccabella olive oil. Over medium heat, sear salmon fillets for a couple of minutes on each side (depending on thickness) until light pink. Remove from pan and set aside.

- For asparagus: Toss all ingredients together in a large bowl and roast on a sheet pan at 425F for 10 – 15 minutes until tender.

stuffed chicken supreme by Chef Alex, Crush Catering

Chef Alex Martin takes chicken to a new level with this Proscuitto-Farmhouse Goat Cheese Stuffed Chicken Supreme with Oyster Mushroom Demi-glace, and Roasted Cauliflower.

Yield 4 servings

1 head of cauliflower (green, orange or white)
2-3 cloves of garlic, peeled and coarsely minced
1 tablespoon lemon juice (or about half a lemon)
Olive oil
Coarse salt and freshly ground black pepper
Freshly grated Parmesan cheese

12 ounces oyster mushrooms
2 tablespoons olive oil
1 red onion, thickly sliced
Dash of salt
1 bay leaf
1 tablespoon chopped garlic
1/4 cup Brandy

3 tablespoons olive oil
4 Airline chicken breasts
4 ounces Farmhouse Goat Cheese
4 Slices of prosciutto, paper-thin
4 ounces roasted red bell pepper(roasted, sliced)
2 ounces arugula
Sea salt, to taste
Black pepper, to taste

For the roasted cauliflower:

- Preheat oven to 400F.

- Lightly oil a large roasting pan or baking sheet. Cut the cauliflower into florets and place them in a bowl. Toss with minced garlic, olive oil, lemon juice. Drizzle with olive oil and toss so that the florets are lightly coated with oil.

- Spread florets, in a single layer, on the roasting pan. Sprinkle with salt and pepper.

- Place the cauliflower in preheated oven, uncovered, for 25-30 minutes, or until the top is lightly brown. Use a fork to test for doneness.

- Remove the cauliflower from the oven and sprinkle generously with Parmesan cheese.

For the oyster mushroom demi-glace:

- In a large sauté pan over high heat, add olive oil. Add the red onion and sauté until tender. Season with salt. Add the mushrooms and bay leaf and cook until mushrooms begin to brown, about 4 to 5 minutes.

- Deglaze the pan with the brandy. Add the garlic and cook for 2 minutes. Add the demi-glace and reduce the heat to medium-low. Let simmer for 10 minutes or until the sauce coats the back of a spoon.

For the stuffed chicken:

- Preheat oven to 350F.

- Place 12-inch cast iron pan over a medium-high heat and add olive oil. Carefully lift the skin on each breast and place ¼ of the goat cheese under each. On top of the goat cheese, layer a slice of Prosciutto and arugula, and then cover by laying the skin back down.

- Season the top and bottom of each breast with salt and pepper. Carefully lay each chicken breast, skin side down, into the pan. Allow the skin to brown for 3 minutes, and then use tongs to turn each breast.

- Place the entire pan into the oven to cook the chicken completely through. This should take about 15 minutes or until the internal temperature is 165F. Serve immediately with roasted cauliflower and oyster mushroom demi-glace.

eat this with...
Adelaida Anna's Red

pickleback fried chicken by Ange Payton, Drink with Experts

This Pickleback Southern Fried Chicken with Whiskey Gravy is a crowd pleaser. Pass the gravy in a sauce boat so your guests can drizzle or drown, depending on their preference.

Yield 6 servings

2 cups dill pickle juice

1 cup buttermilk

Salt & pepper

2 whole chicken, cut in to 8 pieces each

2 quarts oil for frying, canola or peanut

4 cups flour

6 tablespoons baking powder

2 teaspoons salt

½ - 1 teaspoon black pepper

Whiskey Gravy:

2 tablespoons butter

2 tablespoons flour

1/4 cup whiskey

2 cups stock (chicken or vegetable)

2-3 tablespoons Rye whiskey

Salt & pepper

eat this with...
Scottish Breakfast, an oatmeal stout

- Place chicken in 2 large ziplock bags and add one half of the pickle juice and buttermilk into each. Brine the chicken for 4 - 24 hours in the refrigerator.

- Drain the chicken in a large colander and season with salt and pepper.

- Double bag 2 sets of paper lunch bags. Add one half of the following to each bag: flour, baking powder, salt and pepper. Add pieces of chicken, two at a time and shake to coat, switch to new bag after 8 pieces. Use tongs to remove chicken and place on platter. Once all chicken pieces have been coated, let them rest on the platter for 15 - 30 minutes.

- Place a heat proof rack in a baking sheet. Then in a large pot or deep fryer, heat oil to 350 degrees. Begin frying chicken in batches until light golden brown and place on rack. Then place baking sheet with chicken in the oven and bake for 20-25 minutes until done.

- Make the Whiskey Gravy: Melt butter in a medium sized pot. Sprinkle in flour and sauté at least 2-3 minutes. Add whiskey, stirring frequently until it begins to thicken. Add stock and cook 15 minutes. Remove from heat and add 1-3 tablespoons rye whiskey to taste. Season with salt and pepper.

eat this with...
Barrelhouse Mango IPA
Firestone Summer Daze
Tin City Cider

mole poblano by Annie Browne, Hoot 'n Annie

A good mole takes many ingredients to build the flavors. Plan on trying Annie's recipe on a day when you are ready to spend time in the kitchen. Your guests will thank you!

Yield 6 servings

> 3 pounds boneless skinless chicken breasts
> Water to cover
> 8 cloves garlic
> ½ onion, roughly chopped
> Salt to taste

For the sauce:

> 2 tablespoons oil
> 10 -12 ounces dried chilies – anchos, pasillas, mulatos, seeds and membranes removed
> 2 chipotle chilies
> 1 ½ pounds tomatoes, cut in half
> 1 onion, roughly chopped
> 10 cloves garlic
> 5 ounces each, blanched almonds, shelled peanuts, pumpkin seeds, raisins
> 8 whole cloves
> 6 black peppercorns
> ½ teaspoon anise seed
> 2 tablespoons cinnamon
> 3 ounces unsweetened cooking chocolate
> Salt to taste
> Sesame seeds for garnish

- For the Meat: Add the chicken, garlic, and onion to a large sauce pot and cover with water. Boil over medium heat for 45 minutes or until the meat is tender. Remove and set aside. Save the stock for the sauce.

- For the Sauce: Heat 2 tablespoons oil in a large sauté pan. Toast the chilies over medium heat until fragrant. Place them in a large bowl with water to cover. Soak for an hour. Place the chilies in a blender and puree until very smooth. Set aside.

- Place the tomatoes on a cookie sheet and broil until the skins are charred. Remove from the oven and place in a blender with the chipotle chiles. Blend until smooth. Set aside.

- Sauté the chopped onion and garlic in the large sauté pan until soft. Transfer to the blender and puree until smooth. Set aside.

- Sauté the nuts, cloves, peppercorns and anise seed in the sauté pan until fragrant. Transfer to the blender and puree until smooth.

- Add 2 tablespoons oil to a large sauce pan. Add all of the puree into the pot and stir well. Bring to a light boil for 5 minutes. Add 2-4 cups of the chicken stock, cover and cook over low for 20-30 minutes. Add more stock if needed.

- To serve, place the chicken on a plate or platter and smother with a generous amount of the mole sauce. Sprinkle with the toasted sesame seeds.

eat this with...
P.S. Cellars Grenache/Syrah

duck breast by Chef Thomas Drahos, Blue Heron

This duck breast with soba noodle stir fry and sweet, spicy carrot relish is loaded with Asian flavors.

3 tablespoons togarishi powder
1 tablespoon salt
1 tablespoon pepper
8 duck breasts, cleaned, trimmed and scored
1 tablespoon sesame oil
1 red onion, sliced julianne
4 carrots, peeled and diced
4 cloves garlic
1 tablespoon fish sauce
1 tablespoon rice wine vinegar
1 teaspoon honey

1 bunch cilantro, stems removed and finely chopped
1 teaspoon lemongrass puree
3 packs of soba noodles, cooked
1 cup soy sauce
1/4 cup mirin
1 tablespoon sambal garlic chili paste
1 tablespoon palm sugar
1 tablespoon arrow root starch
1 tablespoon tamirand paste
1 pound oyster mushrooms
1 bunch scallions sliced thin

- For the carrot relish: Heat a skillet over medium-high heat, add the sesame oil followed by the diced carrots and cook until tender. Remove from the pan and let cool. Put the carrots, 2 cloves of pressed garlic, fish sauce, rice wine vinegar, honey, cilantro, and the lemon grass puree in and mix until oil is incorporated.

- For stir fry sauce: In a small sauce pot bring to a simmer soy sauce, mirin, sambal chili paste, palm sugar, tamirand paste and 1/2 green scallions.

- For the soba noodle stir fry: Heat a large wok over high heat, add the carrots, onions, the remaining green scallions, and mushrooms. Stir fry over high heat until mixture is slightly reduced, add the prepared sauce, cook for two minutes or until thick. Add the noodles and mix until all ingredients are incorporated.

- For the dry rub: In a mixing bowl mix the togarashi, salt, and pepper. Reserve for duck breast.

- For the duck: Pre-heat the oven to 375F. Heat a large sauté pan over medium heat, when ready season the duck breast with the dry rub and place the duck skin side down, render duck for about 10 minutes slow and low. Flip over and put the duck in the oven for 5 minutes. Remove from the oven and allow the duck to rest for 3 minutes minimum.

- To plate: Place a heaping pile of soba noodles in the middle of a platter, next arrange the duck breast shingling them like cards around the noodles. Spoon the carrot relish around the platter and serve immediately.

eat this with...
LXV Viognier
Tablas Creek Esprit de Tablas

dry duck curry by Neeta Mitta, LXV Wines

This dish from the South of India is best served with hot Basmati rice.

Yield 4-6 servings
  1 full duck (skinned and cut into medium
    pieces and fat removed)

For Marinade:
  1/2 teaspoon turmeric powder
  3 teaspoons red chili powder
  4 teaspoons coriander powder
  4-5 cloves
  1 cardamom
  1 inch cinnamon stick
  2 bay leaves
  1/2 teaspoon whole peppercorns, cracked

For Gravy:
  2 large onions, finely sliced
  2 tomatoes, finely chopped
  4-5 dried whole red chilies,
    each broken into two pieces
  2 teaspoons mustard seeds
  3 curry leaves
  8-10 green chilies, slit lengthwise
  4 tablespoons coconut oil
  2 teaspoons ghee
  1 tablespoon tamarind
  2 tablespoons choppedginger
  2 tablespoons chopped garlic
  1 cup coconut milk

- Marinate the duck pieces with the marinade for at least 2 hours in the refrigerator.

- Heat coconut oil and ghee in a heavy-bottomed pan. Add mustard seeds and when it starts to splutter, add dried red chili, and whole spices. Sauté for a few minutes. Add chopped ginger, garlic, curry leaves, green chilies and chopped onion; sauté until onions turn light brown. Add tomatoes and sauté for a few minutes, until the oil separates from the tomatoes. Add 1/2 cup of water, tamarind, the marinated duck pieces, and salt to taste.

- Cover and cook for 20 minutes or until the duck is half-done, stirring once or twice in between. Remove cover and cook for 5 minutes at high heat until the gravy almost dries up, stirring in between so that it won't stick to the bottom.

- Pour coconut milk over the half cooked duck and adjust the salt. Lower heat and simmer gently until the curry changes to a brown color and oil starts floating on top.

eat this with...
Barrelhouse Brewing Sunny Daze
Donati Family Unoaked Chardonnay
Donati Family Grenache
Four Lanterns Viognier

smoked rabbit faux pho by Richard Verhagen, Hurricane Kitchen

If you don't have a smoker this recipe also works well roasted in the oven.
Richard also makes this dish with duck or chicken legs.

Yield 1 6 servings
- 1 pound rabbit legs
- 2 quarts beef, chicken or vegetable broth
- 2 tablespoon spicy brown mustard
- 2 tablespoons basil pesto
- 8 ounces balsamic vinaigrette
- 12-16 small garlic cloves
- 2 small red onions
- 2-4 Portobello mushrooms
- 2 Pasilla peppers, hulled
- 2 tablespoons olive oil
- 2 teaspoons cumin seed
- 10 ounces soba noodles
- 1/2 cup fresh spinach
- 12 fresh basil leaves
- Fresh mint, to garnish

Rabbit Rub
- 4 tablespoons spicy brown mustard
- 1 teaspoon Montreal steak spice
- 1 teaspoon dried basil
- 1 teaspoon ground Rosemary
- 2 ounces balsamic vinaigrette
- Mix well

- Coat the rabbit legs liberally with the rub.

- Preheat smoker or oven to 225F.

- Place rabbit legs in an uncovered cooking dish and cook until internal temperature reaches 165F. Approximate cooking time: 2 hours for 1 pound of rabbit (checking frequently). Remove rabbit legs and allow to cool. Gently pull all the meat off of the rabbit legs and discard bones. Refrigerate rabbit in a food safe container while preparing other items.

- Pho Broth: In a 4 quart cooking pot, add broth, mustard, pesto, and vinaigrette. Bring to a fast simmer. Allow to simmer for about 5 minutes and set aside.

- Rustically chop garlic, Portobello mushrooms, and peppers. Heat olive oil to medium in a wok and add all chopped ingredients. Add 2 teaspoons cumin seed. Sauté until vegetables are tender, and set pan aside.

- Return broth to burner and heat until boiling. Add noodles and cook until almost done. Add all sautéed vegetables and rabbit to the cooking pot along with spinach and basil. Allow to simmer for approximately one minute.

- Remove from heat and transfer into serving bowls. Transfer noodles first and then ladle out the other ingredients, the broth last. Garnish with fresh mint and serve.

pork loin by Chef Tim Veatch

Pork loin with Tunnato Sauce and Picked Red Onion

Yield 6-8 servings
   2 pound pork loin
   Salt & pepper, to taste
Tonnato Sauce:
   1 cup mayonnaise
   1/2 cup extra-virgin olive oil
   6-ounce can tuna in olive oil (not drained)
   3 anchovy fillets
   2 tablespoons fresh lemon juice
   3 tablespoons drained capers
Quick pickled red onion:
   1 medium red onion, about 5 ounces
   1/2 teaspoon sugar
   1/2 teaspoon salt
   3/4 cup apple cider vinegar

- Preheat oven to 350F.

- Season pork loin liberally with salt and pepper. Roast until internal temperature reaches 145F (approximately 45 mnutes). Remove loin and allow to cool completely.

- In a blender purée all tonnato ingredients, including oil from tuna can, until smooth and season with salt and pepper.

- Whisk first 3 quick pickled ingredients and 1 cup water in a small bowl until sugar and salt dissolve. Place onion in a jar; pour vinegar mixture over. Let sit at room temperature for 1 hour.

- Thinly slice the pork and place on the serving plate. Drizzle the tonnato sauce over the top and add the onions.

chapter 5 - entrées

bourbon smoked pork loin by Richard Verhagen

This recipes requires you to plan ahead since the pork and fruit need 24 hours to absorb all the flavor.

Yield 4-6 servings
- 2 pounds petite pork loin
- 8 fresh figs
- 4 pears
- 4 ounces ginger soy dressing
- Olive oil

For Pork Rub:
- 2 tablespoons paprika
- 1 tablespoon cayenne pepper
- 1 tablespoon onion powder
- 2 tablespoons garlic powder
- 1 tablespoon coriander
- 1 tablespoon black pepper
- 1 tablespoon sea salt
- 1/2 cup bourbon

eat this with...
Lefondusac Grenach Blanc
MCV Wines TMZ
Donati Family Pinot Blanc
Penman Springs Dry Humour

DAY 1

- Combine all pork rub ingredients with pork in a refrigerator-safe bag and seal. Refrigerate for at least 24 hours.

- Slice 4 pears and 6-8 fresh figs. In a refrigerator-safe bag, combine pairs, figs, and store-bought ginger soy dressing. Refrigerate for 24 hours.

DAY 2

- Preheat oven to 350F.

- Pork: Add 2 tablespoons of olive oil to a wok or large sauté pan and heat to medium high. Oil a baking sheet large enough for the pork. Remove pork from the refrigerator and from the marinade. Carefully sear pork on all sides in the wok or sauté pan.

- Add pork, sliced figs and pears to the baking sheet. Bake until the pork's internal temperature reaches 165F. Remove pork from the oven and allow to rest for approximately five minutes.

- Simultaneously remove figs and pears from the baking sheet and transfer to serving plates. Slice pork on a bias and serve over figs and pears.

sheppards pie by Lisa Pretty

You can make this recipe in a large casserole dish, individual ramekins or oven-safe soup bowls. This is another comfort food dish that is perfect for a fall or winter dinner.

- Place potatoes in medium sized pot. Cover with water, add a teaspoon of salt, and bring to a boil. Reduce to a simmer, and cook until tender (about 20 minutes).

- While the potatoes are cooking, melt 4 tablespoons of the butter in a large sauté pan on medium heat. Add the chopped onions and carrots, cook until tender, about 6 to 10 minutes.

- Add beef, lamb, and Worcestershire sauce. Cook, stirring occasionally, until the meat is no longer pink. Season with salt and pepper. Add corn and peas, broth, thyme and cumin. Bring to a boil, then reduce heat to simmer. Cook uncovered for 10 minutes, adding more beef broth if necessary to keep the meat from drying out.

- When the potatoes are tender, remove from heat and drain liquid. Add remaining 4 tablespoons of butter, mash with a potato masher, and season with salt and pepper to taste.

- Pre-heat oven to 400F.

- Layer the ingredients in oven proof baking dish(es) staring with the meat mixture, then the mashed potatoes, with cheese on top.

- Bake in oven until browned and bubbling, about 30 minutes. If necessary, broil for the last few minutes to help brown the cheese.

Yield 6 servings

3 large russet potatoes, peeled and quartered
8 tablespoons (1 stick) butter
1 medium onion, chopped
2 cups vegetables—diced carrots, corn, peas
1 pound ground beef
1/2 pound ground lamb
1 tablespoon Worcestershire sauce
1/2 cup beef broth
1 tablespoon dried thyme leaves
1 teaspoon cumin seed
Salt and pepper to taste
2 cups grated Gruyère cheese

eat this with...
Brecon Estate Cabernet Franc
Caliza Azimuth
Cass Rockin' One Red
Castoro Merlot
Penman Springs Petit Verdot
San Marcos Creek Cabernet Franc
Windward Pinot Noir

lamb chops
by Chico Mora, The Catch Seafood Bar and Grill

The secret to Chef Chico's lamb chops is his overnight marinade.

Yield 4 servings
1 rack of lamb
1/2 cup olive oil
1 tablespoon minced garlic
Juice of one lemon
Juice of one orange
1 tablespoon Kosher salt
1 tablespoon pepper

- Combine all ingredients in a sealable container and marinate overnight in the refrigerator.

- Heat broiler. Remove lamb from marinade and place on a sheet and broil approximately 8 minutes per side. Allow rack to rest 5 minutes prior to cutting into chops.

eat this with...
Penman Springs Petit Verdot

rack of lamb by Tablas Creek

This garlic & herb crusted rack of lamb makes a hearty entrée. The folks at Tablas Creek recommend serving these on a bed of butternut squash puree with a side of ratatouille.

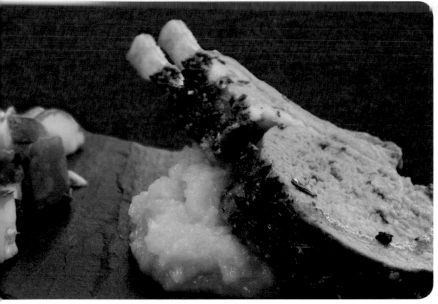

eat this with...
Tablas Creek Esprit De Tablas

Yield 4 servings
> 1 rack of lamb
> 6-8 cloves of garlic, peeled & finely chopped
> 6 sprigs of Rosemary, finely chopped
> 1-2 tablespoons olive oil
> Salt & pepper, to taste

- Combine garlic and Rosemary in a small bowl. Season the lamb generously with salt and pepper, then coat with the garlic Rosemary mixture. Leave the coated lamb at room temperature for 30 minutes to marinate.

- Preheat oven to 450F.

- Place lamb on aluminum foil lined baking sheet and bake for 12-15 minutes. Rotate the lamb and cook for an additional 8-10 minutes

- Remove lamb from oven and allow to rest on a cutting board, covered, for 10 minutes. After resting, slice into chops and serve.

pulled beef chili verde by Darian Buckles, Templeton Hills Beef

When making pulled beef recipes, it is important to use cuts of beef that shred well. Templeton Hills Beef recommend a front shoulder roast such as an O-bone.

Yield 6-8 servings
2-3 pound roast: chuck, O-bone
2 tablespoons olive oil
Salt & pepper to taste
1 small onion, minced
½ bunch cilantro, minced
16 ounces green salsa (hot, medium, or mild)
12 ounces light beer

- Pre-heat oven to 300F.

- Rinse and pat roast dry, season with salt and pepper. In a stove-to-oven pan, heat olive oil until hot, sauté onions and cilantro until onions are golden.

- Place meat in pan and sear both sides, approximately 3-4 minutes a side. Pour salsa and beer over meat, bring to a boil. Place lid on pan and put pan in oven. Cook 2 3 hours until meat shreds easily.

- Remove pan from oven. Remove meat from pan and allow to cool until able to handle. Using two forks, shred meat. Return meat to pan. May cool and refrigerate until next day. Heat or reheat on stove top. Serve with tortillas, rice, beans, cilantro, lettuce or cabbage.

eat this with...
Barrelhouse Juicy
Graveyard Tombstone Red
Penman Springs Merlot
Polmar Junction Merlot
Riverstar Zinfandel
San Marcos Creek Benniolo
Seven Oxen Zinfandel
Tin City Cider

wine country sandwich by Angela Payton

These sandwiches take a little time to prepare; however, they are worth the effort. You can substitute bread dough or biscuit dough if you are not a puff pastry fan. Almost any homemade or store bought dough works great.

Yield 4 servings
- 2 sheets puff pastry
- ½ teaspoon sca salt
- Freshly ground cracked black pepper
- 1 egg, whipped for egg wash

Steak Filling:
- 10-ounce Ribeye steak
- ½ ounce blue cheese (Gorgonzola, Maytag, Stilton)
- 1 cup sliced mushrooms
- 1 tablespoon butter
- ½ teaspoon fresh thyme
- ¼ teaspoon white truffle oil (optional)
- 2 tablespoons finely diced shallots
- Salt and pepper

eat this with...
Brecon Estate Petite Sirah
Cass Cabernet Sauvignon
Graveyard Petite Sirah
JUSTIN Justification
Pomar Juction Merlot
Ranchero Cellars Revolver
Riverstar Affinity
Seven Oxen Tannat
Tablas Creek Terret Noir
Windward Pinot Noir

- **To prepare the filling:** Over medium-high heat, sear the steak in a hot skillet, remove from skillet and place on cutting board to rest. In the same skillet, melt 1 tablespoon of butter. Add the sliced mushrooms and stir to coat with melted butter. Sauté until mushrooms are golden brown (approximately 5 minutes).

- In a glass bowl, add the mushrooms, fresh thyme, cheese, salt and pepper. Stir until the cheese has melted.

- Preheat oven to 350F

- **To create the sandwiches:** Place a puff pastry sheet on a large baking sheet covered with parchment paper. Place the mushroom mixture down the middle third of the pastry, being careful to leave a ¼ inch space at the top and bottom. Drizzle with truffle oil, if desired.

- Slice the steak into thin strips and layer on top of the mushroom mixture.

- Cut ½ to 1 inch horizontal strips into the pastry, evenly, along both sides of the filling. Starting with the left top strip, fold it across the filling at a slight angle and lightly press the end at the base of the top right side strip. Fold the right top strip over the previous strip and filling, then press it at the base of the next left strip. Repeat until all but the bottom two strips are braided down the sandwich. Brush these with egg wash and wrap around the bottom to seal. Brush egg wash and crimp to seal the top edge. Brush egg wash over sandwich then sprinkle with sea salt, freshly cracked pepper, and shallots on top.

- Repeat the above steps to create the second sandwich. Bake in oven for 25-30 minutes, until golden brown.

- Cut each sandwich into two pieces. Can be served hot, warm or room temperature.

hanger steak with citrus pesto by The HATCH

This hanger steak is all dressed up with rub and citrus pesto. The rub can be stored for up to a month in an airtight container, so you may want to make a double batch. Feel free to add extra garnish to your platter.

Yield 6 servings
>   2-2.5 pounds hanger steak
>   Olive oil
>   Salt & pepper

Citrus Pesto:
>   1 tangerine, peeled, cut into sections and chopped
>   1 lime, peeled, cut into sections and chopped
>   1 orange, peeled, cut into sections and chopped
>   1 bunch Italian parsley, finely chopped
>   1 cup baby arugula, chopped
>   Kosher salt

BBQ Rub:
>   1 tablespoon cumin
>   2 tablespoons fennel
>   2 teaspoons cinnamon
>   ½ cup brown sugar
>   4 tablespoons chile powder
>   1 tablespoon paprika
>   1 tablespoon kosher salt

- For rub: Whisk all ingredients in a small bowl.

- For pesto: Combine all ingredients in a medium bowl.

- Rub steak with ½ cup BBQ rub and grill on medium heat for 4-5 minutes per side for medium rare. Remove from the grill and let rest for 5-10 minutes before thinly slicing.

- Serve on a big platter with pesto dotted and drizzled over meat and around the plate. Optional: sprinkle with additional rub.

eat this with...
Riverstar "Affinity"

filet mignon

by Chef Alma Ayón, Sundance Bed & Breakfast

The green peppercorn cream sauce really makes this dish! Make this for special occasions or just a delicious mid-week meal.

Yield 4 servings

- 4 6-8 ounce beef tenderloin medallions
- Salt & pepper, as needed
- 1 tablespoon butter
- 1 tablespoon olive oil
- 3 shallots, chopped
- 2 cloves of garlic, minced
- ¾ cup Brecon Cabernet Franc
- 1 cup beef stock
- ¼ cup heavy cream
- 1 tablespoon green peppercorns

Alma Ayón is the Resident Chef and co-owner of the beautiful Sundance Bed & Breakfast in Paso Robles. After more than 20 years as a Live Events and Emmy Award-Winning Television Producer, Alma decided to leave television behind and follow her passion for cooking by enrolling in the Le Cordon Bleu College of Culinary Arts in Hollywood. After graduating with Honors, she worked in fine restaurants and catering companies in LA before visiting and falling in love with Paso Robles and the Central Coast. Chef Alma now serves unique three-course gourmet breakfasts at Sundance daily and on Saturday nights her guests can also experience fine dining with a multi-course dinner paired with wonderful Central Coast wines!

- Preheat oven to 350F.

- Season beef medallions with salt and pepper. Heat oil and butter on high heat in a heavy saucepan. Sear beef medallions on all sides and transfer to sizzle plate. After the green peppercorn sauce has been made, finish cooking the beef in oven until internal temperature reaches 135F for medium rare (about five minutes depending on thickness). Let rest for 3-5 minutes before plating.

- Using the same pan used to sear the beef (medium heat), add shallots and sauté until golden brown (do not burn). Add garlic and wine and cook until wine has cooked off almost completely. Add beef stock and boil until liquid is reduced by half. Strain and transfer to another pan and continue cooking with medium heat. Add cream and peppercorns and cook until sauce coats the back of a wooden spoon (about 10-15 minutes). Season with salt and pepper if needed. Keep warm.

- Place beef medallion in the center of a plate and spoon green peppercorn sauce on top and around. Serve with potatoes, carrots or any vegetables of your choice.

eat this with...
Brecon Estate Cabernet Franc
Brecon Estate Syrah

prime rib by J&R Natural Meats

This Prime Rib with Rosemary Salt Crust is the perfect recipe when you have a large group for a special dinner. In addition to sourcing the prime rib from J&R Meats, FARMstead ED recommends Windrose Farm, The Groves on 41 and Spice of Life for other local ingredients.

Yield serves 12 (with leftovers)
 1 whole boneless rib eye (12 to 15 pounds)
 Extra virgin olive oil
 1/4 cup tri-color peppercorns
 5 sprigs fresh thyme
 3 sprigs fresh Rosemary
 1/2 cup minced fresh garlic
 1/2 cup kosher salt

- Preheat the oven to 450F.

- Coarsely grind peppercorns. Shed and rough chop the leaves from the thyme and Rosemary sprigs. Mix salt with the crushed peppercorns, Rosemary leaves, thyme leaves and garlic. Polish the roast with oil and rub on the herb & garlic mix, patting slightly for it to stick to the meat. Set into roasting pan with rack. Roast for 20 minutes, then reduce the heat to 275F, further roasting until a meat thermometer registers 125F for rare/medium-rare (approximately 3-4 hours, depending on roast size). Remove from the oven and let rest for 15 to 20 minutes before slicing (the roast will continue to cook slightly after removing from the oven).

eat this with...
Rangeland Cabernet Sauvignon
Adelaida Version Red
Brecon Estate Cabernet Sauvignon
Caliza Companion
Cass Reserve
Glunz Family Cabernet Sauvignon
JUSTIN Isoseles
Penman Springs Petit Verdot
P.S. Cellars It's Intense
Ranchero Cellars Carignan
Riverstar Affinity
Seven Oxen Zinfandel
Tablas Creek Mourvèdre

pan seared venison by Annie Browne, Hoot 'n Annie

The bacon jam is a wonderful complement to the seared venison. Annie recommends serving the venison over gorgonzola hash browns (see her recipe on page 47).

Yield serves 4
- 4 venison steaks or chops
- 1/3 cup olive oil
- 1/3 cup orange juice
- Juice of one lemon
- 3 garlic cloves, crushed
- 2 sprigs Rosemary
- 4 tablespoons bacon fat

For bacon jam:
- 1 onion, fine dice
- ½ pound bacon
- 2 tablespoons apple cider vinegar
- 3 tablespoons honey

- In a Ziplock bag, combine olive oil, juice, garlic and Rosemary. Add the venison to the bag and make sure each steak/chop is well covered. Zip bag shut, removing as much air as possible and place in the refrigerator. Marinate for several hours, or overnight if possible.

- For the bacon jam: Par cook the bacon in a sauté pan, just until it starts to firm up. Chop the bacon into small pieces. Drain all but a few tablespoons of the bacon fat out of the sauté pan and reserve for searing venison. Add the onion and sauté until it starts to caramelize. Add the bacon and sauté for a couple of minutes. Add the vinegar and honey and simmer for about 5-10 minutes.

- In a large skillet, heat the reserved bacon fat over medium high heat. Remove the venison from the marinade and add to the skillet. Discard marinade. Sear venison on each side to brown well. Depending on the thickness, cook 4-5 minutes on each side or until medium.

- Serve topped with bacon jam.

eat this with...
Polmar Junction Cabernet
Brecon Petite Sirah
Broken Earth Petit Verdot
Castoro Cellars Merlot
Glunz Family Winery Zinfandel
JUSTIN Justification
Ranchero Cellars The Hive
Seven Oxen Tannat
Tablas Creek Mourvèdre

eat this with...
Cass Cabernet Sauvignon

wine braised short ribs by Chef Jacob, Cass Café

Chef Jacob recommends serving these ribs over mashed root vegetables and braised kale with crispy pancetta. Don't forget to spoon plenty of sauce over the top.

Yield 6 servings

5 pounds bone-in beef short ribs, cut crosswise into 2-inch pieces
Kosher salt and freshly ground black pepper
3 tablespoons vegetable oil
3 medium onions, large dice
3 medium carrots, peeled, large dice
2 celery stalks, large dice
1 jalapeno, seeded, chopped

5 cloves garlic, roughly chopped
1 tablespoon tomato paste
750 ml Cass Cabernet Sauvignon
4 cups beef stock
10 sprigs flat-leaf parsley
8 sprigs thyme
4 sprigs oregano

- Preheat oven to 350F.

- Season short ribs with salt and pepper. Heat oil in a large Dutch oven over medium-high. Working in 2 batches, brown short ribs on all sides, about 8 minutes per batch. Transfer short ribs to a plate. Pour off all but 3 tablespoons drippings from pot.

- Add onions, carrots, jalapeno, and celery to pot and cook over medium-high heat, stirring often, until onions are browned, about 5 minutes. Add garlic and sauté for 2 minutes more. Add tomato paste and herbs. Cook, stirring often, until well combined and deep red, 2-3 minutes. Stir in wine, allow to boil for 2 minutes to burn off the alcohol, then add short ribs with any accumulated juices. Add stock and bring to a boil. Cover, and transfer to oven.

- Cook until short ribs are tender. Check this by jabbing a fork into a couple of them. There should be no resistance. Should take 2–2½ hours, maybe longer depending on size of short ribs. Transfer short ribs to a platter. Strain sauce from pot into a measuring cup. Spoon fat from surface of sauce and discard; season sauce to taste with salt and pepper if needed.

braised boneless short ribs by Ryan Swarthout, Paso Robles Inn

Chef Ryan recommends serving these braised short ribs over creamy polenta and topped with roasted carrots.

Yield 4 servings

1.5 pounds short ribs
2 tablespoons extra virgin olive oil
Salt and pepper to taste
½ large yellow onion, diced
3 cloves garlic, minced
2 tablespoons tomato paste
2 cups red wine
2 bay leaves
⅔ cup water
¼ cup fresh parsley, chopped, for garnish

eat this with...
Graveyard Vineyards Cabernet Sauvignon
Graveyard Vineyards Petite Sirah
Graveyard Vineyards Scream

- Preheat oven to 225F.

- Heat olive oil in pan over medium heat.

- Generously season all sides of the short ribs with salt and pepper. Add short ribs to hot oil and sear for 2-3 minutes on each side until short ribs are browned on the outside. Remove short ribs from pan and set aside.

- Add onion and garlic. If the pan looks too dry, add another splash of olive oil. Sauté 2-3 minutes until onion is translucent. Add tomato paste and stir to combine. Add red wine to pan to de-glaze. Make sure to scrape any browned bits off the bottom of the pan with a wooden spoon! Add bay leaves and water to pan and stir to combine. Bring the mixture up to a low simmer, then remove from heat.

- Add short ribs back to the pan, nestling them in with the onions. Cover pan and bake in oven for 3-4 hours.

chapter 6 - desserts

citrus granita with agave by Chef Jacob, Cass Café

This light and refreshing dessert is the perfect ending for any meal. You may even want to serve this in between courses as a palate cleanser.

Yield 4-6 servings
> 2 cups fresh squeezed orange juice
> ½ cup fresh squeezed lime juice
> ½ cup fresh squeezed red grapefruit juice
> 1 cup agave syrup
> 8 sprigs, fresh mint

- In a large bowl, mix the three juices with the agave syrup until well blended. Pour into a 13x9 pyrex cake pan and freeze for 30 minutes.

- Using a fork, agitate the granita. Continue this procedure for the next 3 hours, fluffing and stirring with a fork every thirty minutes.

- Prior to service, give it one final stir, then scoop into bowls and serve immediately. Garnish with a mint sprig.

eat this with...
Cass Late Harvest Roussanne

wine-poached figs by Amy Butler, Ranchero Cellars

Pairing a dry white wine with dessert can be tricky. Amy nailed the pairing with wine-poached figs and honey-Chèvre cream. Be sure to make extra as your guests may want seconds.

Yield 4 servings
- **½ bottle Ranchero Cellars Chrome**
- **2 tablespoons sugar**
- **2 tablespoons honey**
- **2 3-inch sprigs fresh thyme, plus more for garnish**
- **4-5 black peppercorns**
- **10-12 plump fresh figs, destemmed and halved lengthwise**

- **6 ounces fresh Chèvre, softened**
- **2 tablespoons honey**

- In a saucepan, mix the wine, sugar, and honey until sugar is dissolved. Add thyme sprigs and peppercorns and bring mixture to a boil. Simmer 5 minutes, then add figs. Continue to cook over low heat for another 5 minutes, or until figs are soft and the syrup has begun to thicken. Remove figs; continue to simmer until the syrup is reduced by half, about another 5 minutes. Allow to cool to room temperature.

- Cream Chèvre and honey with an electric mixer until fluffy.

- Pipe Chèvre cream into serving dishes and top with figs and wine syrup. Garnish with more fresh thyme.

eat this with...
Ranchero Cellars Chrome

shortbread cookies by Barbara Goodrich, Hartley Farms

Raspberry lemon shortbread cookies are a fun treat to serve with wine after dinner or even as a decadent afternoon snack.

Yield approximately 12 four-inch cookies
- 2 tablespoons Hartley Farms Raspberry Preserves
- 1 cup Butter
- ½ teaspoon almond extract
- 2 ½ cups all-purpose flour
- ½ cup granulated sugar
- 1/8 teaspoon salt

Powdered Sugar Icing
- 1 cup powdered sugar
- 1 tabelspoon lemon juice
- ¼ teaspoon almond extract
- 1 tablespoon Hartley Farms Raspberry Preserves
- Milk

- Pre-heat oven to 325F.

- In a large bowl, mix all cookie dough ingredients. Kneed dough until smooth; form dough into a ball.

- Roll dough to ¼-inch thickness on a lightly floured surface. Cut out dough using cookie cutter (whatever shape you like). Place cutouts 1 inch apart on ungreased cookie sheet.

- Bake 12-16 minutes or until edges just start to turn brown. Transfer cookies to a wire cooling rack. Cool completely.

- Mix first 4 powdered sugar icing ingredients together, along with enough milk to make a drizzly icing.

- Drizzle cookie tops with icing. If desired, sprinkle with coarse sugar. Let stand until icing is set.

eat this with...
Adelaida The Don
Four Sisters Kekoa
Graveyard Deliverance
Paso Port Brandi Zin Port
Pear Valley Bom Final
Riverstar Twilight

lemon olive oil cake by The Groves on 41

This moist lemon olive oil cake is a wonderful dessert to serve with a glass of wine. You can dress it up with whipped cream, fresh mint, berries, drizzle with The Groves on 41 Royal Raspberry Olive Oil, or simply serve a slice on its own..

Yield 8-10 servings
3/4 cup The Groves on 41 Meyer Lemon Olive Oil
1 large lemon, juice and zest
1 cup cake flour
5 large eggs, separated
3/4 cup sugar (1/2 + 1/4)

eat this with...
Cass Late Harvest Roussanne
Glunz Family Winery Mission Angelica
Graveyard The Ascender
Penman Springs Trembler Trois
P.S. Cellars It's SWEET
Tablas Creek Sacrérouge

- Set rack in middle of oven; pre-heat to 350F.

- Grease pan and line with parchment paper.

- In small bowl, whisk together lemon zest and cake flour.

- In another bowl beat egg yolks and ½ cup of sugar, approximately 3 minutes on high until thick & pale. Reduce to medium speed and add olive oil and lemon juice until combined.

- Fold together yolk mixture and flour mixture with wooden spoon (do not beat).

- In separate bowl beat egg whites at medium speed with salt until foamy; slowly add ¼ cup of sugar, continue beating until egg whites hold soft peaks, estimated 3 minutes. Gently fold 1/3 egg white mixture into yolk mixture, then fold in remaining egg white mixture. Pour batter into pan, gently rap pan on surface twice to release air bubbles.

- Sprinkle 1 1/2 teaspoons of sugar on batter

- Bake for about 45 minutes, until puffed and golden. A pick or skewer inserted in center comes out clean.

- Cool cake in pan on rack for 10 minutes. Run a knife around the edges; then release the side of the pan. Cool cake to room temp (approximately 45 minutes). Remove bottom of pan and parchment paper and transfer cake to serving platter.

panna cotta by FARMstead ED

Panna Cotta with Drunken Berry Compote is a fairly easy recipe to make, that will be sure to impress your guests. FARMstead ED recommends sourcing ingredients from these local producers: Talley Farms, Stepladder Ranch, Windrose Farm, and Straus Family Dairy

Yield 8 servings
- ¼ cup cold water
- 2 ½ teaspoons unflavored gelatin (2 packets)
- 3 cups heavy whipping cream
- 1/3 cup honey + 3 tablespoons
- 1 whole vanilla bean; split

Drunken Berry Compote
- 4 ½ baskets fresh berries (raspberries/blackberries)
- 1/3 cup white port
- Fresh mint for garnish

- Pour ¼ cup cold water into small custard cup. Sprinkle in gelatin over top of water. Let stand until gelatin softens, about 10 minutes. Bring 1 inch water in small skillet to boil. Place cup with gelatin in water. Stir until gelatin dissolves, about 2 minutes. Remove from heat.

- Combine cream, vanilla bean and 1/3 cup honey in medium heavy saucepan. Stir over medium heat until honey dissolves. Remove from heat. Remove vanilla bean. Mix in gelatin. Divide mixture amongst 8 wine or port glasses. Cover and chill until set, at least 6 hours and up to 1 day.

- Combine berries and 3 tablespoons of honey in medium bowl. Crush berries lightly with back of spoon. Mix in port. Let compote stand until berry juices & honey form light syrup; stir often. Make 1-2 hours ahead.

- Spoon berries over panna cotta and garnish with fresh mint sprig.

eat this with...
Paso Port Angelica
Cass Late Harvest Roussanne
Vines on the Marycrest Rosé

crème brulee cheesecake by Ryan Swarthout, Paso Robles Inn Steakhouse

Loaded with vanilla flavor, this crème brulee cheesecake is a decadent dessert. For an added touch, garnish the serving plates with caramel sauce.

Yield 8 servings

1 refrigerated rolled pie crust (from a 15-ounce package)
3 (8 ounce) packages cream cheese, room temperature
1 1/3 cups sugar
1 vanilla bean
1/4 teaspoon salt
1 1/2 cups heavy cream
10 large egg yolks
2-3 tablespoons superfine sugar

- Preheat the oven to 325F.

- Prepare a 9-inch spring form pan. Tear off an 18-inch square of heavy duty aluminum foil. Set the pan in the center of the square and carefully wrap the foil up over the edges of the pan, crimping at the top so that it is secure. Repeat with a second sheet of foil. Be very gentle so it doesn't tear. Repeat again with a 3rd sheet of foil. Press pie dough into the spring form pan.

chapter 6 - desserts

- In a large bowl or stand mixer, beat the cream cheese for 4 minutes, making sure to scrape the sides. Add sugar and salt, beat for another 4 minutes, scraping sides. Add the cream and scraped vanilla bean to a small pot on the stove. Heat over medium low heat until it is warm. You don't want it to boil.

- Place egg yolks into a mixing bowl. Beat the egg yolks for about 2 minutes, until they are pale. While the beaters in the egg yolks are on, slowly add the warm cream. Once all of the hot cream has been incorporated with the egg yolks, it's time to slowly pour that into the cream cheese mixture.

- Beat the cream cheese and slowly pour in the egg-cream mixture. Make sure you scrape the sides and beat until there are no lumps. The batter will be pretty thin. Transfer the foil-wrapped crust into a large high-sided skillet, or a roasting pan. Pour the batter into the pie dough, forming an even layer on top. Fill the skillet or roasting pan with HOT water from the tap. You want the water to go at least halfway up the pan of the cheesecake.

- Carefully transfer the water bath to the oven. Bake for about 1 hour and 35 minutes. You will know it is done when it is mostly set in the center and doesn't jiggle too much when you shake it.

- At this point you can either crack the door of the oven or let the cheesecake come to room temperature inside the oven.

- When the cheesecake is mostly cool, remove from the water bath, and remove the foil. Cover the cheesecake with plastic wrap and refrigerate for at least 3 hours or preferably overnight.

- When you are ready to serve, remove the plastic wrap and carefully loosen the sides of the pan.

- Sprinkle about 2 tablespoons superfine sugar all over the top of the cheesecake.

- Use the torch to caramelize the sugar. Let sit for a minute for the sugar to harden.

eat this with...
Graveyard Estate Syrah
Graveyard The Ascender
Graveyard Deliverance

don's heavenly fruit tart by Donn Exterkamp & Cinquain Cellars

Don Exterkamp, of San Miguel, is the winner of the Cinquain Cellars Dessert Cook-Off, and he shares his recipe here. If you don't have the fruit listed, no problem! Just go with whatever you have that is fresh and in season. It's sure to be delicious sitting atop the buttery, flaky tart crust and delectable cream cheese filling

Yield 6-8 servings

For the crust:
- 3/4 cup butter, softened
- 1/2 cup powdered sugar
- 1-1/2 cups all purpose flour

For the filling:
- 11 ounces vanilla baking chips, melted
- 1/4 cup whipping cream
- 8 ounces cream cheese softened

For the fruit topping:
- 2 kiwis, peeled and sliced
- 1 pint raspberries
- 1 pint blackberries

For the glaze:
- 3 tablespoon sugar
- 2 teaspoon cornstarch
- 1/2 teaspoon lemon juice

- Pre-heat oven to 300F.

- Cream butter and sugar together, gradually add flour, mix well. Press into ungreased 11-inch tart pan. Bake for 25 to 30 minutes or until golden brown and firm to the touch. Set aside to cool.

- Beat chips and cream. Add cream cheese, beat until smooth. Spread over crust. Chill for at least 30 minutes, then arrange fruit on top.

- Put all glaze ingredients in a sauce pan and bring to a boil, let cool and brush or drizzle over fruit. Place in refrigeration and bring to room temperature just prior to serving.

eat this with...
Cinquain Cellars Touriga and Tinto Cao
Four Sisters Sparkling Wine
Graveyard Vineyards Deliverance
P.S. Cellars - It's SWEET
Pear Valley Frizzante
Penman Springs Muscat Blanc
San Marcos Creek White Merlot

gingerbread by Darian Buckles, Wine Diva Jams

This gingerbread with a rum and jam glaze smells as good as it tastes! Although it is perfect with Spiced Syrah Jelly, you can substitute your favorite jam or jelly.

Yield 8 servings

1 ½ cups flour
½ cup sugar
½ teaspoon baking soda
½ teaspoon baking powder
½ teaspoon salt
1 teaspoon ground ginger
1 teaspoon ground cinnamon
1 teaspoon ground allspice
¼ teaspoon ground nutmeg

¼ cup butter, melted
¼ cup molasses
½ cup sour cream
1 egg, well beaten
8 ounces Wine Diva Spiced Syrah Jelly
1/3 cup dark rum

- Preheat oven to 350F. Grease a nine inch cast iron pan.
- In bowl combine flour sugar, baking soda, baking powder, and all spices. In a second bowl combine egg, molasses, butter, sour cream, whisk until blended. Combine dry mixture with wet mixture, until smooth and creamy. Place in prepared pan. Bake for 30-35 minutes until cake springs back lightly from sides of pan. After removing cake from oven, poke holes in cake using a skewer or fork. Pour glaze over top. Allow to cool for 10 minutes before serving.
- To make glaze, cook jam/jelly and rum together, stirring often, until jam has melted and mixture is thick but smooth. Pour over cake.

eat this with...

Adelaida Muscat Blanc
Cass Late Harvest Roussanne
Glunz Family Winery Mission Angelica
Graveyard The Ascender
Paso Port Havana Port
Penman Springs Muscat Blanc
Pear Valley Pretty Girls
Riverstar Syrah Rosé
San Marcos Creek Late Harvest Zinfandel
Seven Oxen Zinfandel

chocolate truffles by Tablas Creek

These chocolate truffles are easy to make and are great for a sweet ending to any meal....or even as a mid-day treat with a glass of dessert wine.

Yield 48 truffles

2 cups bittersweet or semi-sweet chocolate chips
1 ¼ cups heavy cream
1/2 cup chopped walnuts
1/2 cup sifted cocoa powder

Note: you can substitute your favorite toppings for the walnuts and cocoa powder

- In a small saucepan over low heat, warm cream. When warmed, remove pan from heat, stir in chocolate, whisking until smooth and creamy. Spread chocolate mixture into a shallow pan and refrigerate for 2 hours.

- Using a small melon baller, measure and roll truffles. Coat in desired toppings.

- Chill until ready to serve.

eat this with...
Tablas Creek Sacrérouge
(Mourvèdre Vin de Paille dessert wine)

jam tarts by Darian Buckles, Wine Diva Jams

Darian has several winning combinations of ingredients for these tarts. Pick one that sounds good to you or create your own.

Jam Shortbread Tart Combinations

Apple/Carmel/ Hot Cinnamon Candies/Maple Chips/Walnuts
Apricot/Almond/Pecan
Chocolate/Almond/Hazelnut/Heathbar Crumbles/Peppermint
Peach/Almond/Maple Chips/Spiced Pecans
Hot Zin/Cheese
Strawberry/Hot Cinnamon Candies/Maple Chips/Pecans

Any Flavor Combination YOU like Works!

eat this with...
Glunz Family Winery Mission Angelica
Graveyard The Ascender
Pear Valley Belle Fin
Penman Springs Trembler Trois

Yield 8 servings
12 tablespoons butter, softened
½ cup sugar
¼ teaspoon flavoring of choice
1 ½ cup flour
1/8 teaspoon salt
1 jar jam/jelly
Nuts/candy of choice

- Pre-heat oven to 350F.

- Cream sugar and butter, add flavoring. Add flour & salt. Set aside ½ cup of mixture. Press into 9x9 inch tart pan. Spread softened jam over top, sprinkle set aside dough and nuts/candy over jam.

- Bake 40-50 minutes.

chocolate mousse bombes by Chef Alma Ayón

These Chocolate Mousse Bombes with Raspberry Coulis are a little bit of work; however, the end result is worth all the effort. These little bombes by Chef Alma Ayón are sure to impress your guests. Alma makes these as a special treat for guests at her Sundance Bed & Breakfast.

- Preheat oven to 375F.

- Spray sheet pan with Pam, or butter with pastry brush. Cut a piece of parchment or wax paper and line the bottom of the sheet pan. Spray the surface of the paper lightly and up the sides to prevent cake from sticking.

- Sift dry ingredients (except granulated sugar): cake flour, cocoa powder, confectioners sugar and baking powder. In a large bowl mix canola oil, eggs, almond extract, hazelnut paste until well combined (about 2 minutes).

- Add dry ingredients in two parts at low speed until well combined. In a separate bowl mix egg whites and granulated sugar to form soft medium peaks (about 5-7 minutes). Fold egg white mixture gently into batter, one-third at a time. Pour batter onto prepared sheet and bake in middle rack of oven until set (about 20-25 minutes).

- Remove from oven and let cool completely on a rack. To remove, place sheet upside down on a flat surface and peel off parchment paper.

Yield 12 servings

For the chocolate chiffon cake:
   (makes one 12x17 sheet pan cake)
   5 ounces cake flour
   1 ½ ounces cocoa powder
   4 ½ ounces confectioners sugar
   1 ½ teaspoon baking powder
   3 ½ ounces milk
   3 ounces canola oil
   2 small eggs
   1 teaspoon almond extract
   1 ounce hazelnut paste (or Nutella)
   6 ounces egg whites
   4 ½ ounces granulated sugar
   Pam spray or soft butter

chapter 6 - desserts

For the chocolate mousse:
    6 ounces semisweet chocolate, chopped
    ¼ cup milk
    2 ounces butter
    2 ounces Brecon Petite Sirah
    1 egg yolk
    1 cup heavy cream, cold

- Place a bowl inside a pan of simmering water (low-medium heat), making sure the bowl fits snuggly over the pan and the bottom does not touch the water. Melt together chocolate, milk, Petite Sirah and butter in the bowl. Using a rubber spatula stir gently until completely melted. Remove bowl from pan and set aside to cool to lukewarm temperature. Whisk in the egg yolk. In a separate bowl whip the heavy cream to medium peaks and fold it gently into chocolate mixture until fully incorporated. The mixture should now look and have the consistency of chocolate mousse.

For the raspberry coulis:
    12 ounces bag frozen raspberries, thawed
    3 tablespoons granulated sugar
    2 tablespoons water (or orange juice)
    Fresh raspberries for garnish

- Using a blender, mix all ingredients at high speed for 45-60 seconds. Strain to remove seeds. Refrigerate coulis in an airtight container until ready to serve.

Chef Note: *Using tempered chocolate is important in order to obtain a crispy and shiny chocolate dome. Chocolate is in temper between 88-91F.*

For the chocolate dome:
    12 ounces semi-sweet chocolate, tempered
    12 silicon hemisphere molds (2 ¾" diameter)

- With the chocolate in temper, using a pastry brush, brush the inside of the silicon molds and put in refrigerator for about five minutes to harden the chocolate before applying another coat. Repeat this step two more times until you have applied three coats of chocolate in each mold (let the chocolate harden completely between coats).

- **To assemble the bombes:** Using a 3 inch round cutter, cut out 12 rounds from the chocolate chiffon cake. Fit a pastry bag with a plain tip and fill with chocolate mousse. Pipe mousse into chocolate molds about 2/3 full. Gently top each mold with a round of chiffon cake. Freeze molds until firm (about 3 hours). Transfer molds to refrigerator.

- **To service:** Un-mold the bombes onto a lined cookie sheet by peeling the silicon mold one by one. You can keep covered in refrigerator until one hour before service. Bring to room temperature before serving. For plating, place 1-2 tablespoons of raspberry coulis at the bottom of the plate, then place one bombe in the center and garnish with fresh raspberries.

eat this with...
        Brecon Estate Petite Sirah

chocolate mousse cakes by Alex, Crush Catering

*These baked dark chocolate mousse cakes with salted caramel sauce
will delight any chocolate lover!*

Yield 6-8 petite cakes
> **3.5 ounces dark chocolate (bittersweet 85%)**
> **1.7 ounces semi sweet chocolate**
> **3.5 ounces unsalted butter**
> **1 medium egg**
> **1 teaspoon pure vanilla extract**
> **1.7 ounces raw sugar (or Castor)**

Salted Caramel Sauce
> **1 cup granulated sugar**
> **1/2 cup heavy cream**
> **2 tablespoons unsalted butter**
> **3/4 teaspoon kosher salt**

Prepare Salted Caramel Sauce

- In a medium saucepan set over medium-high heat, combine the sugar with 1/4 cup cold water and stir to combine. Cook, without stirring, until the sugar has turned a deep amber hue, approximately 10 to 12 minutes.

- Meanwhile, warm the cream in a small saucepan. When the caramel is ready, slowly whisk in the warm cream and continue simmering the mixture until it is smooth, another 2 to 3 minutes. Remove from heat, then whisk in the butter, and then the salt, to taste. Serve warm.

chapter 6 - desserts

- Preheat the oven to 300F.

- Spray muffin tins (silicon works best) with non stick cooking spray.

- Place chocolate and butter in a heat proof bowl and microwave for 1 minute. Repeat for 10-15 seconds if necessary until the chocolate is completely melted. Set aside and allow chocolate mixture to cool for about ten minutes.

- In a separate bowl, beat the egg and sugar together with an electric hand beater or mixer until the eggs form a ribbon when the beaters are lifted out of the bowl. This will take about ten minutes.

- Pour the slightly cooled chocolate mixture and fold gently into the whisked egg mousse using a rubber spatula. Be careful not to over stir.

- Divide the batter between the molds. Bake for eight minutes near the top half of the oven.

- Allow to cool completely before placing in the fridge to chill. Gently remove the mold when ready to serve.

- Smear warm caramel sauce on plate, place mousse cake on top. Optional: garnish with cherries, cream. mint and lavender.

eat this with...
Adelaide Zinfandel

chapter 7 - cocktails

Austin Sanderson, Fish Gaucho
Austin has been bartending for many years and is known for his speed. His creativity is expressed through his unique cocktails. He likes to play with flavors that play well together -- especially the ones that others say won't work!

Young OG by Austin Sanders
- 1 oz grapefruit juice
- 2 oz orange juice
- 1 oz simple
- ½ oz blood orange (Simple)
- 2 oz tequila

Shake grapefruit guice, simple, tequila. Strain over ice. Sink blood orange to bottom of glass.

Mo' Honey No Problems by Austin Sanders
- 1 ½ oz Lemon
- 1 oz Rosemary-Black Pepper-Honey
- 1 ½ oz Tequila
- ½ oz RE:FIND Rye

Shake all ingredients. Strain over big ice block.

Kryptonite by Austin Sanders
- 1 ½ oz RE:FIND Gin
- ½ oz Chartreuse
- ¼ oz Midori
- ½ oz Simple (Kiwi/Rosemary)

Shake all ingredients. Double-strain into coupe. Top with Graveyard Cellars Ascender sparkling wine.

All Gold Everything by Austin Sanders
- 1 ½ oz Oro Azul
- ¾ oz 43
- ½ oz honey
- ¾ oz lemon
- ½ oz pineapple habanero salsa
- Splash of St. Germain

Shake all ingredients. Double-strain into coupe. Top with sprite and soda, lemon zest salt.

Briana Lonien, The HATCH

Briana has been bartending since the day she turned 21. She makes the classic drinks from muscle memory. For her, bartending is fun, especially creating unique cocktails that bring people together.

Local Talent by Briana Lonien

Briana was inspired to make this cocktail because of the amount of delicious Luxardo cherry juice left over after using the cherries in Old Fashioneds and Manhattans at The Hatch. What stemmed from her love of Luxardo cherries and inability to toss out their juice is this bright and crisp cocktail that is great to enjoy any time of day.

> 2 oz Krobar Gin
> 1/2 oz fresh grapefruit juice
> 1/4 oz fresh lemon juice
> Drizzle of Luxardo cherry juice
> 2 dashes SLO Bitter Co. lavender bitters
> 3 oz Cass Sparkling

Shake grapefruit juice, simple, tequila. Strain over ice. Sink blood orange to bottom of glass.

Rye² by Briana Lonien
Cocktails don't need to be solely spirit based! This cocktail utilizes a delicious local whiskey and one of Briana's favorite local beers.

> 1 oz RE:FIND rye whiskey
> 1/2 oz Averna
> 1/2 oz Giffard Banana liquor
> 1 oz fresh orange juice
> 2 oz BarrelHouse Brewing Co. Rye IPA
> 2 dashes Angostura bitters

Shake all ingredients except the IPA and strain over a large ice cube in a rocks glass. Top with the IPA and garnish with a banana chip.

Fallen Apple by Briana Lonien
Almost magically, this simple cocktail came together almost on the first try. It just goes to show how important good ingredients are to the creation of great drinks!

> 2 oz Cinnamon Wine Shine
> 1/2 oz unfiltered apple juice
> 1/2 oz Rosemary infused simple syrup
> 1/2 oz fresh lime juice

Shake all ingredients and strain into collins glass filled with ice. Garnish with 3 thin slices of apple and a cinnamon stick.

chapter 7 - cocktails

Lavender 75 by Yes Cocktail Co.
1 oz Yes Lavender Honey mixer
1 oz Krobar Gin
Top with Graveyard Vineyards Sparkling Wine

Combine mixer and gin in a shaker on ice, and then strain into a champagne flute. Top with sparkling wine.

Yes Cocktail Co. was founded by Lauren and Brandon Alpert in 2015. Frustrated with artificial corn syrup filled mixers found at most liquor stores, Lauren and Brandon decided to create their own. With the bountiful harvest of the central coast at their disposal, they took to the farmer's market and the rest is history. Inspired by the classics, handcrafted for the modern bar, Yes Cocktail Co. has mixers and syrups for all of your mixology needs.

Hibiscus Rose Sour by Yes Cocktail Co.
1.5 oz Yes Hibicus Rose mixer
2.5 oz Krobar Rye Whiskey
1 egg white

Shake ingredients in a cocktail shaker with ice, strain into a chilled coupe, garnish with a Rose petal, and serve.

Bitter Kiss by Yes Cocktail Co.
1 oz Yes Grapefruit Thyme mixer
1 oz RE:FIND Vodka
2 dashes Angostura Bitters
Top with Cass Sparkling Wine

Shake mixer, vodka and bitters in a shaker over ice. Strain into a champagne flute and top with bubbly.

Ginger Smash by Yes Cocktail Co.
1.5 oz Yes Ginger Citrus mixer
1.5 oz RE:FIND Rye
5 Mint Leaves

Combine the ingredients in a cocktail shaker. Muddle the mint in. Add ice and shake. Stain and serve over an old fashioned glass filled with crushed ice.

The Cocky Rooster by Yes Cocktail Co.
2 oz YES Sriracha Lime mixer
1.5 oz RE:FIND Rye
5 Mint Leaves

Salt the rim of a pint glass. Combine ingredients in a pint glass and stir. Garnish with a Jalapeno slice.

Casey Biggs, Paso Wine Man

Casey may be known as the Paso Wine Man, but he loves his chilled beverages. On his first trip to Italy, over 15 years ago, he discovered Negroni and has since perfected his recipe. He enjoys going to Krobar since he can get all the ingredients in one stop.

Negroni by Casey Biggs

Negroni is known as the cocktail that destroyed a generation after the 1st world war.

1 oz Krobar Gin
1 oz sweet vermouth
1 oz compari

Pour over ice, and stir all ingredients together. Casey likes to pour a floater of Absinthe for a kicker of flavor -- this is known as a "Quill". He prefers his Negroni on the rocks, garnished with orange rind.

Joe Barton, Krobar Distillery

Joe, owner/winemaker of Barton Family Wines, has been in the wine industry since his youth. He only started enjoying cocktails 6 years ago, and for him, they need to be interesting and all alcohol - he doesn't enjoy mixers. He took first place at the California Craft Spirit Competition, so he clearly knows his stuff. He is co-owner of Krobar Distillery with Steve Kroener.

Barkro by Joe Barton
Hmmm...Joe may have wanted his name first in the combined distillery name. At least he got to name this drink!

> 2 oz Krobar Gin
> .5 oz Krobar neutral brandy
> .5 oz Krobar LIT
> Rosemary for garnish

Shake ingredients and pour neat. Garnish with Rosemary.

Lemon Splash by Scott Howenstine
*Scott created this cocktail recipe during a dinner party
I attended - it was a hit!*

    1 oz RE:FIND Vodka
    .5 oz RE:FIND Limoncello
    .5 oz lemon juice
    .5 ox orange juice
    .5 oz simple syrup
    Splash soda
    Splash 7up
    Thyme to garnish

Shake all liquid ingredients, strain and pour neat.
Garnish with thyme.

Sparkling Holiday Cocktail by Kelly Marie Baldal
*Kelly made this cocktail at a friend's holiday party. I
was so impressed I asked her to share her recipe.*

2 oz Opolo Sparkling Wine
1 ½ oz Absolute Vanilla Vodka
½ oz cranberry juice
Lemon twists
Fresh cranberries

Add sparkling wine to your champagne flute. Add
vanilla vodka. Slowly float the cranberry juice on top.
Garnish with lemon twist and fresh cranberries.

Orange Fizz by Pendray's Distillery

> 2 oz Pendray's Orange Liqueur
> 1 oz Hanger 1 Vodka
> 1.5 oz Fresh Orange Juice
> Ginger Ale

In a shaker combine Pendray's Orange Liqueur, Hanger 1 Vodka and fresh orange juice. Shake with ice, strain into a glass, add a splash of Ginger Ale, garnish with an orange wedge.

Plum Spritzer by Pendray's Distillery

> 3 oz Pendray's Plum Liqueur
> 1 oz Hanger 1 Vodka
> 1.5 oz Cranberry Juice
> Angostura Bitters
> Sparkling Water

In a shaker combine Pendray's Plum Liqueur, Hanger 1 Vodka, cranberry juice and 3 dashes bitters. Shake with ice, strain into a glass, add a splash of sparkling water.

The Steve Hates It! by Pendray's Distillery

> 1 oz Pendray's Orange Liqueur
> 1 oz Pendray's Walnut Liqueur
> .5 oz Pendray's Grappa

Mix straight into a glass!

TEMPLETON
— CALIFORNIA —
PENDRAY'S
DISTILLERY
— EST. 2014 —

Pendray's Distillery, owned by Steve and Lola Glossner, is named after Lola's maiden name and originating from Cornwall England, 'Pendray' which is Cornish, is a race of people with a rich Celtic heritage and an indomitable fighting spirit who inhabited the Southwest of England.

Having a distillery was always part of their business plan and in 2013, they purchased a 500 liter German pot still from Holstein. Pendray's Distillery produces spirits for sipping, mixing and fortifying their port wines.

Orange Nutcracker by Pendray's Distillery

> 1.25 oz Bourbon
> 1/2 oz Cocchi Vermouth di Torino
> 1/2 oz Pendray's Walnut Liqueur
> 1/2 oz Pendray's Orange Liqueur
> 2 Dashes Fee Brother's Orange Bitters
> Stirred with ice

In a shaker combine all ingredients. Shake with ice and strain into a glass, garnish with an orange slice.

French 45 by Lisa Pretty

How can you go wrong when the recipe includes gin and sparkling wine?

2 oz Krobar Gin
1/2 oz fresh lemon juice
4 oz Opolo Sparkling Wine
Lemon rind for garnish

Pour gin and lemon juice in a Champagne flute. Top with sparkling wine and serve with a lemon twist.

Hot Chocolate Wine by The Chocolate Stache
This is a great way to use up your left over wine!

1 box Chocolate Stache Mexican hot chocolate bark
2 cups almond milk
1/2 bottle red wine

In a medium sauce pan, over medium heat, combine broken chocolate pieces and almond milk. Whisk over heat, until a thick chocolate milk is formed. Add in red wine, while continuing to whisk until mixture is warm.

Serve in glass mugs. Top with whipped cream and grated chocolate for a beautiful presentation.

S'Mores Cocktail by Graveyard Vineyards

Deliverance Dessert Wine
Marshmallow Vodka (chilled)
Fine Graham cracker crumbs
Marshmallow cream
Garnish: Toasted Marshmallows on a skewer

Coat the rim of a martini glass with marshmallow cream then dip in graham cracker crumbs.

In a cold shaker, pour equal parts Deliverance and marshmallow vodka and shake. Pour into martini glass. Place toasted marshmallows on a skewer and place as garnish on the glass.